I0514187

Title: The Litlle book of the abstract universe. What do you see?

Abstract Universe Collection Nª1

Author: Marian Muñoz

Texts: Marian Muñoz

Cover Design: Marian Muñoz

Editorial Design: Marian Muñoz

Editorial Layout: Estudio Branding Esencial

Diagramming: Marian Muñoz

Edition and writing: Marian Muñoz

Translated by Maria Palop

© Mariángeles Muñoz, 2019

brandingesencial@gmail.com

First edition

Madrid – Spain 2019

Website: www.brandingesencial.com/

Special edition for Amazon.com

ISBN: 9781792839085

All rights reserved. Total or partial reproduction of this work it is not allowed, nor its incorporation into a computer system, nor its transmission in any form or by any means (electronic, mechanical, copy, recording or other) without its prior written authorization from the copyright holder Marian Muñoz.

The Little Book Of
the abstract universe

WHAT DO YOU SEE?

The Little Book Of
the abstract universe
WHAT DO YOU SEE?

MARIAN MUÑOZ

edition Amazon

Prologue

Dear reader, I am proud that my book is in your hands, recovering meaning through your eyes.

This book is read with the eyes, but can only be understood with the chemistry between brain and heart.

You have in your hands a visual experience, a journey into the complex visual construction that the mind gives us.

In this book you will find food for the imagination. An entertaining discovery about how we can see what is not, but it is, in multiple ways. Meanings constructed by the observer's psychic.

Colors, textures, geometry, strokes and composition will allow you to travel through this curious exhibition, find mysterious, fun, dramatic, nostalgic, tender and surreal scenarios.

As the author, from three works "Where everything emerges", "Where everything springs" and "Where everything is manifested", created with mixed techniques: watercolors, acrylic and markers, I have extracted different visual meanings that only each observer can build. Without a doubt, only a few.

"The little book of the abstract universe" is an invitation to create your own scenarios. Do your work, transform it, reconstruct it and play with meaning and meaning at your whim. You are the starring in this work.

My enormous curiosity as the creator of this work, leads me to ask myself: What do you see?

About the original works

Each print was created with a previous study of the colors that have been used.

As the designer evolved in each one of the works, she let herself be carried away by the strokes and colors she felt she had to choose.

Without other pretension than to express herself through color, shapes and overlapping textures, the personality of each painting was created.

Acrylic inks, watercolors and markers have been used on a basis of newspapers and magazines chosen for the textures of its paper Couche, fine and delicate, which involved continuous drying times for each layer and strokes used in order to avoid mixing the different colors.

This small creative book does not try to show abstract technique or transmit knowledge of art, but to give the possibility to play and create by the observer through his own feeling when looking at each centimeter of the different plates.

Each work allows the option of creating micro frames of independent fragments and discarding those that do not tell us anything, as shown a few pages later in "Adaptation of original works to personalized prints and pictures":
For any query or specific request about the work, you can contact with brandingesencial@gmail.com.

This is the first issue of a collection of copies of "The Little Book of the Abstract Universe. What do you see?" very different but created with the same approach: Play and mentally find meanings with the forms and abstract compositions that are proposed.

About the Author

Marian Muñoz is an independent graphic designer, creator of "Essential Branding" and the visual blog ESENCIAL.

After many years dedicated to the care work, she found her passion for design after a vital and professional expedition of the most disconnected at the time.

Passionate about editorial design, the creation of image branding and illustration, her design philosophy lies in "seeing beyond the visible" and transferring it to the graphic atmosphere of each assignment regardless of your nature.

She has developed her own creative process so she defines herself as a constant learner, devourer of books and in constant training.

She is conceptually considered an "Indie" designer, with a humanist tendency in her way of posing and doing design, however, very respectful of the theories and the fundamentals of graphic design that allowed her to learn.

She builds the image branding, develops and designs an editorial concept, creates book covers, posters or logos, starting from a complex and original way of exploring the initial Briefing with her clients in each project.

Her extensive knowledge and interest in human psychology, personal development and various methods of emotional exploration allow her to go beyond the limits of a conventional Briefing and to excavate aspects that are unnoticed and considered essential to be present and transmitted on the graph of every job.

She is an advocate of the "Indie concept" with a free, flexible graphic design and without fear of breaking the established rules when necessary, replacing them with what we like and attract, rather than graphically correctness.

You can learn more about her in her portfolio and website www.brandingesecial.com

To my visual readers

Original Works

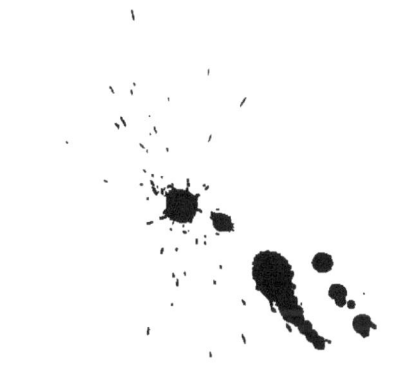

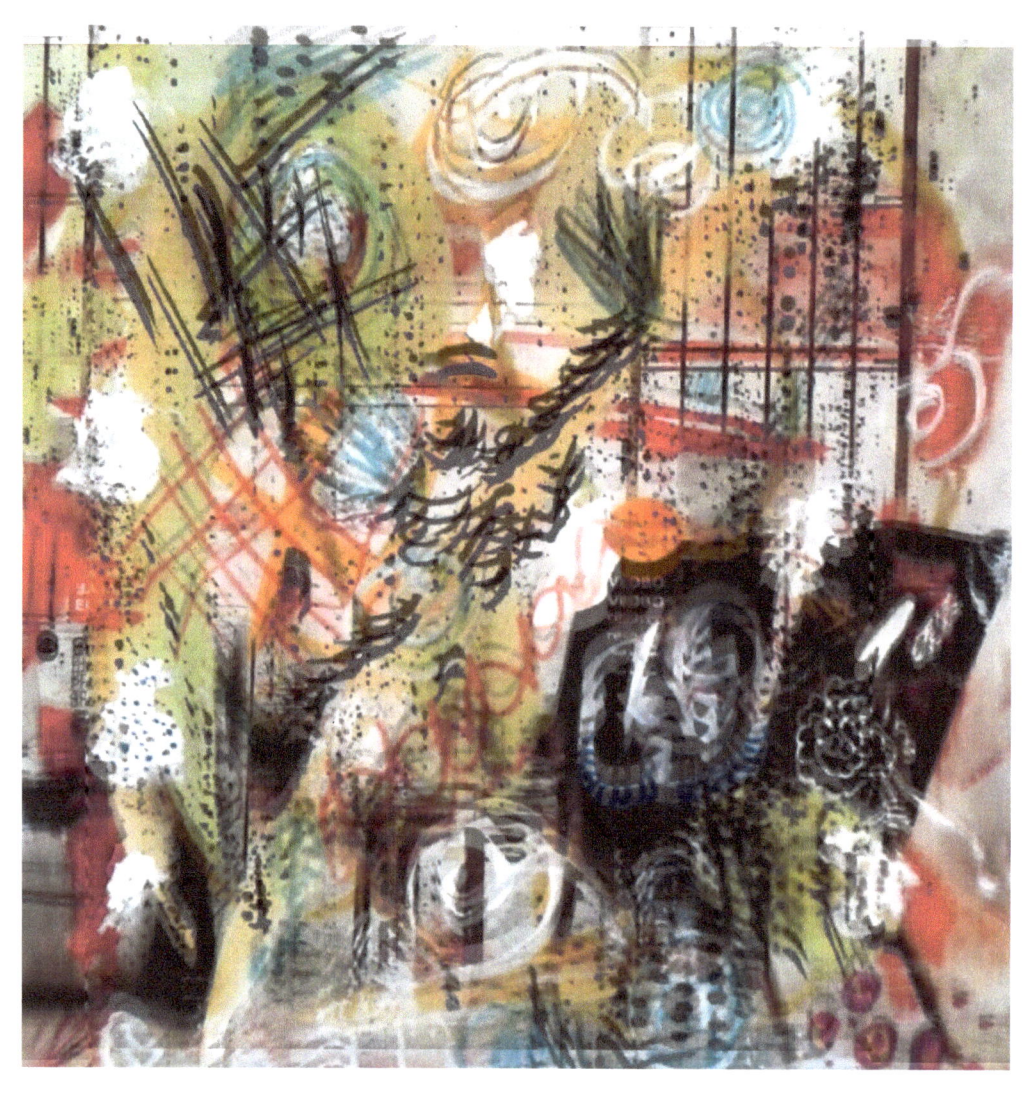

WHERE EVERYTHING SPROUTS
WHERE EVERYTHING SPROUTS

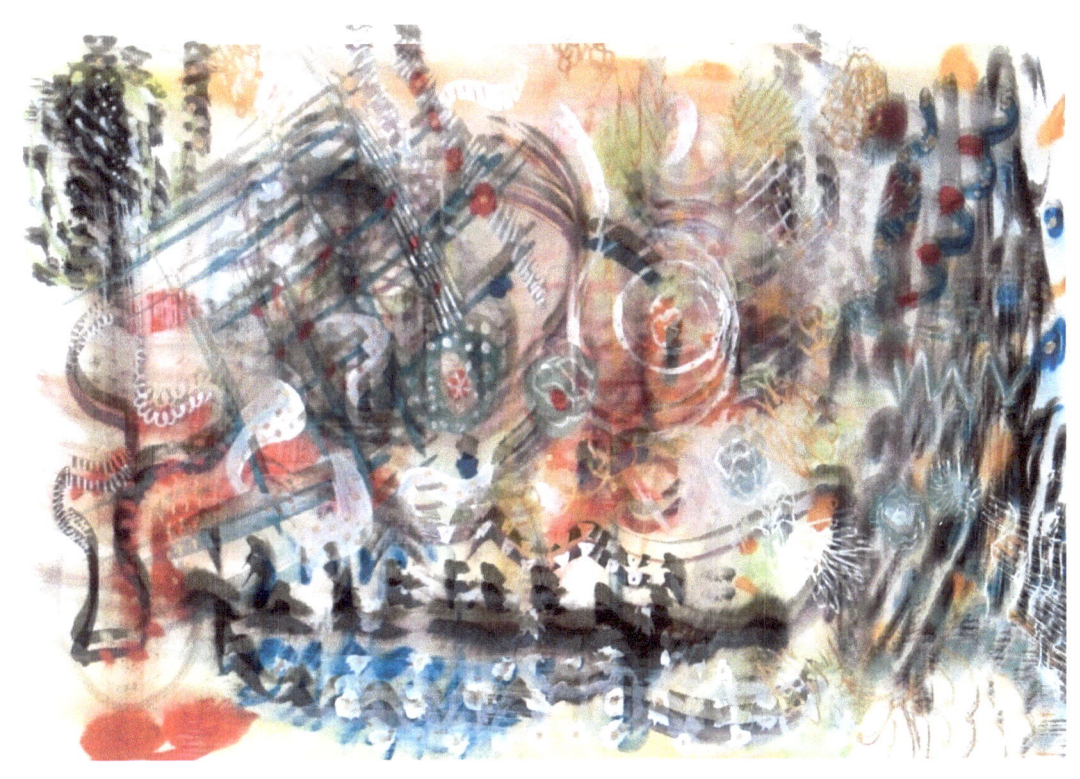

WHERE EVERYTHING EMERGES

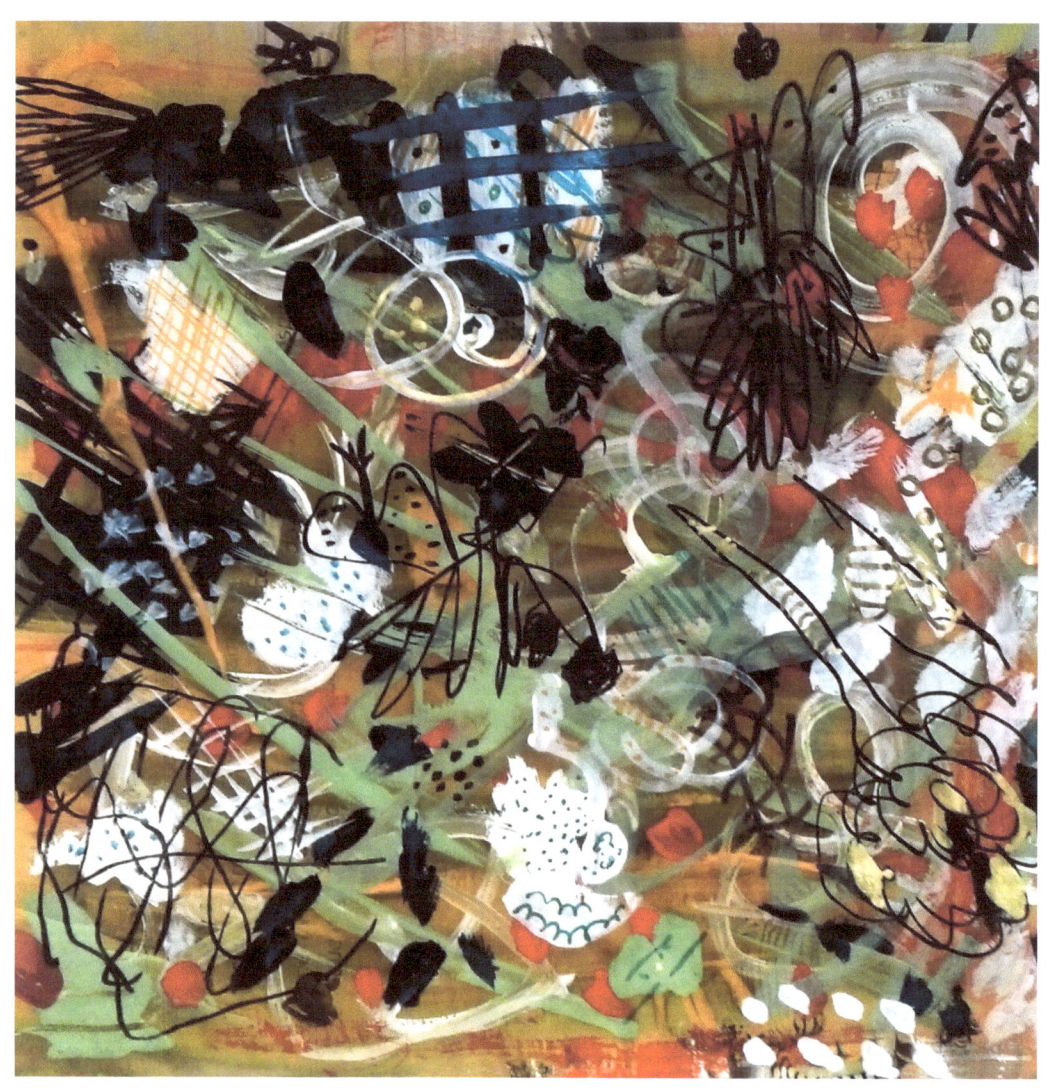

WHERE EVERYTHING IS MANIFESTED

ADAPTATION OF ORIGINAL WORKS

ADAPTATION OF ORIGINAL WORKS

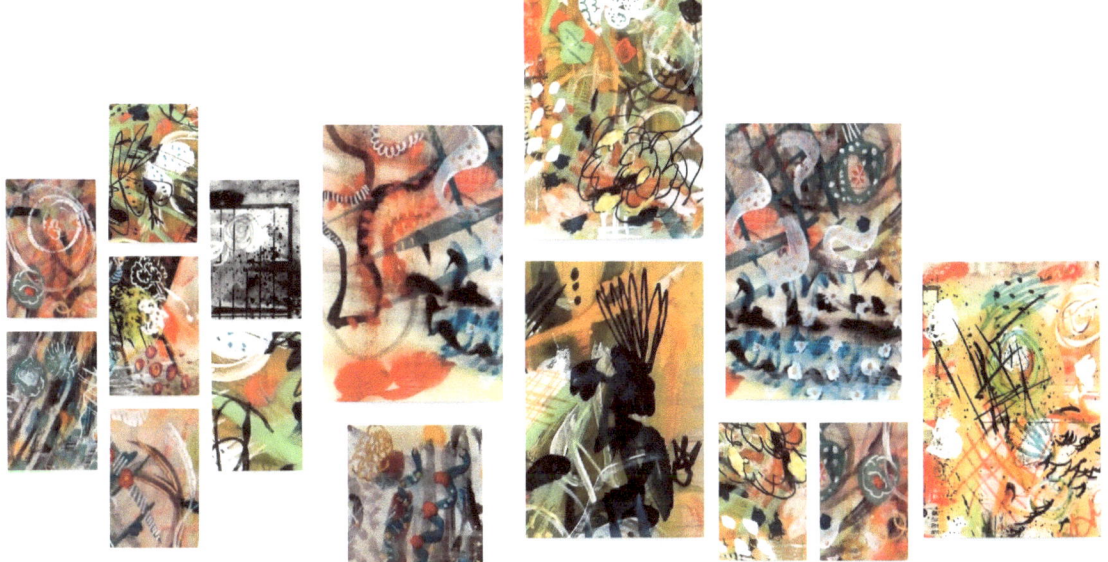

YOU CAN HAVE A PERSONALIZED PRINT SELECTING A FRAME YOU LIKE AND PERSONALLY ORDERING IT TO THE AUTHOR AT:
pedidosbrandingesencial@gmail.com

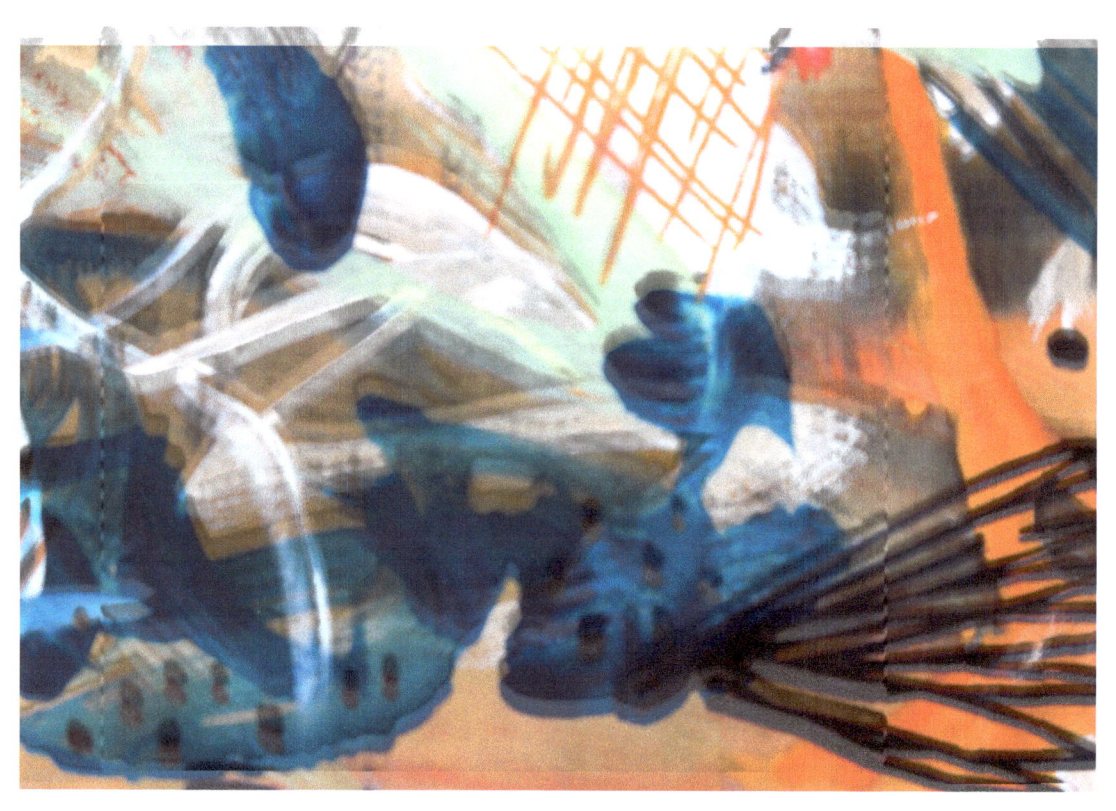

FISHES MEETING
FISHES MEETING

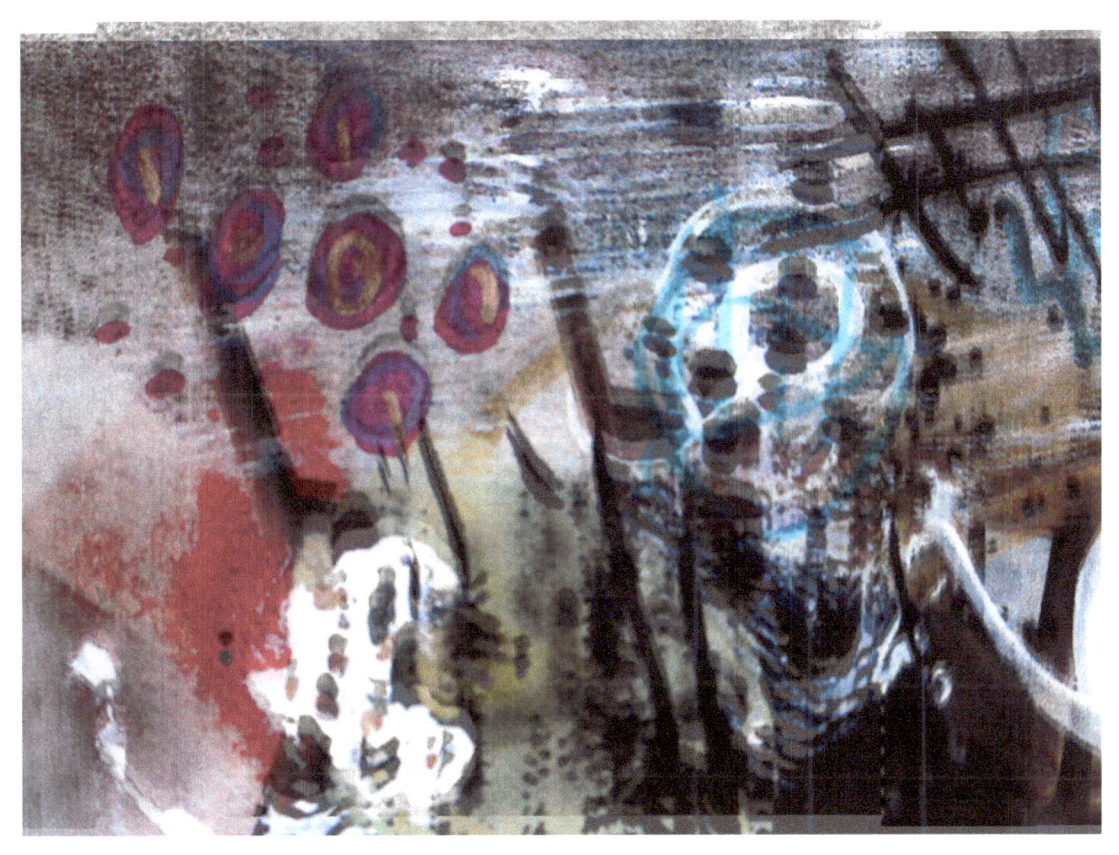

THE HURRICANE IS COMING
THE HURRICANE IS COMING

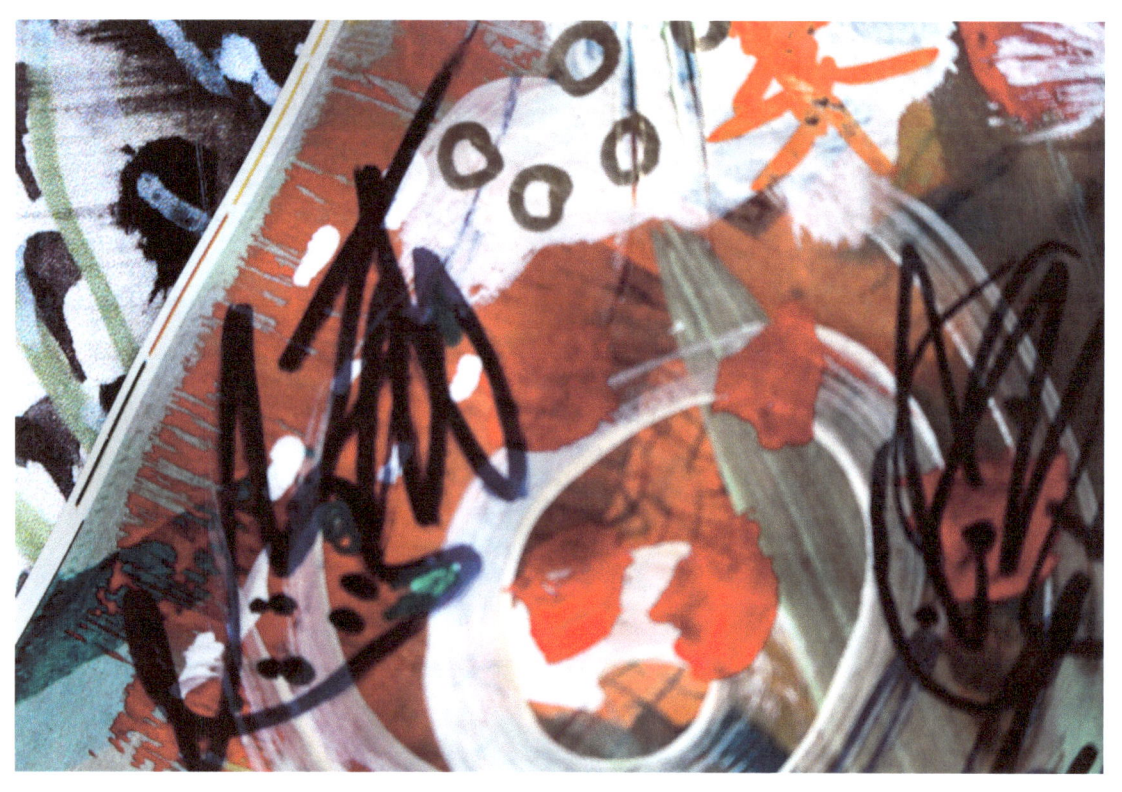

BNEST OF HAPPY BIRDS

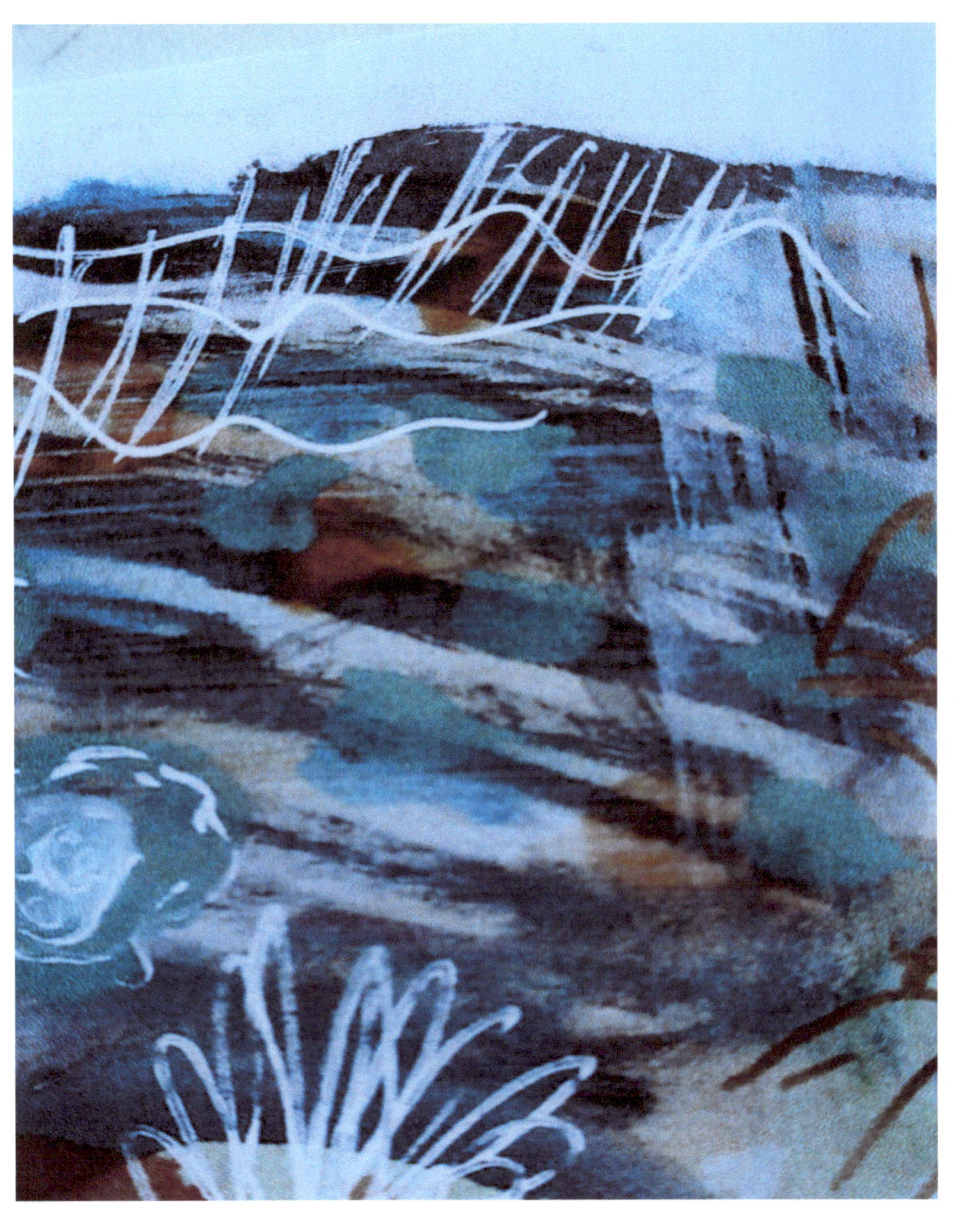

ROUGH SEA

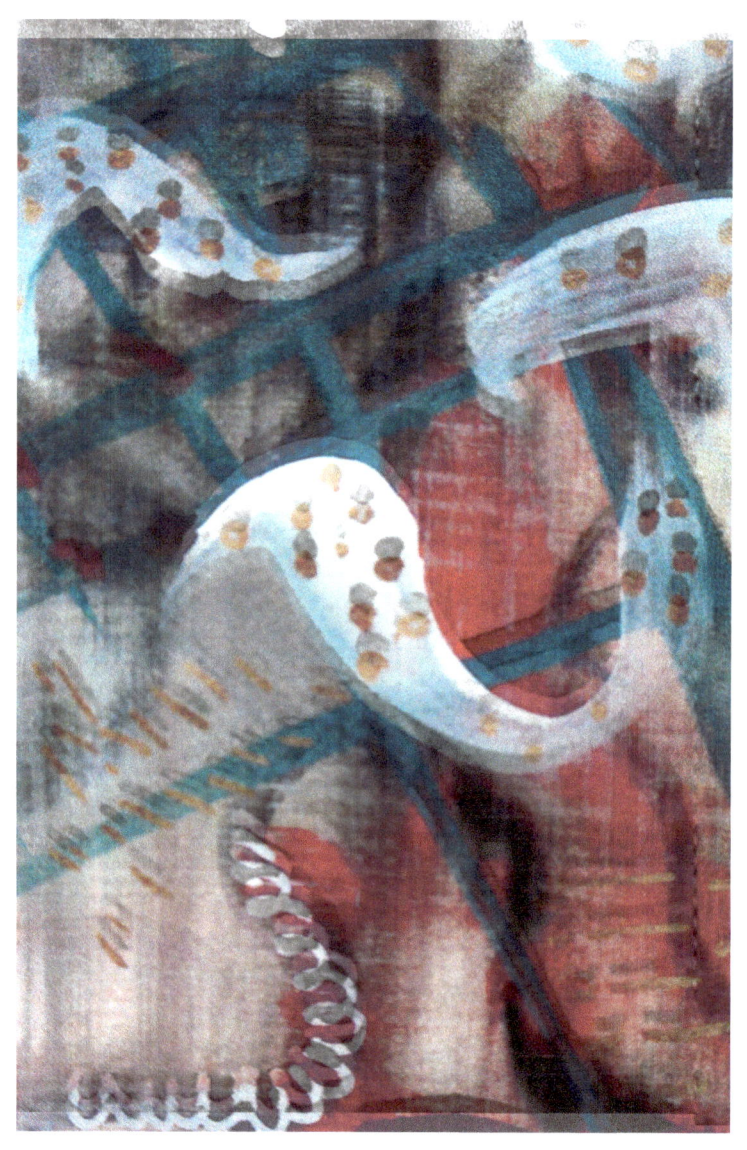

JAILED GHOSTS

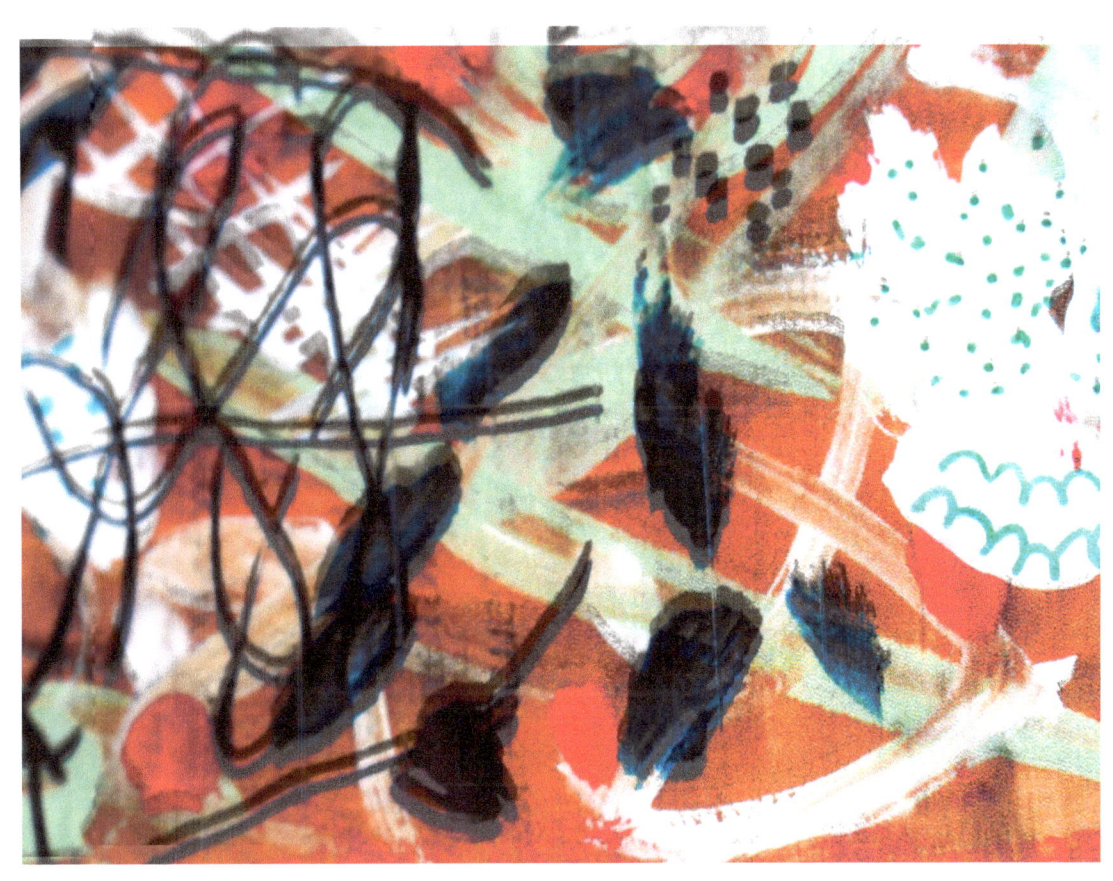

DOWNED FEATHERS
DOWNED FEATHERS

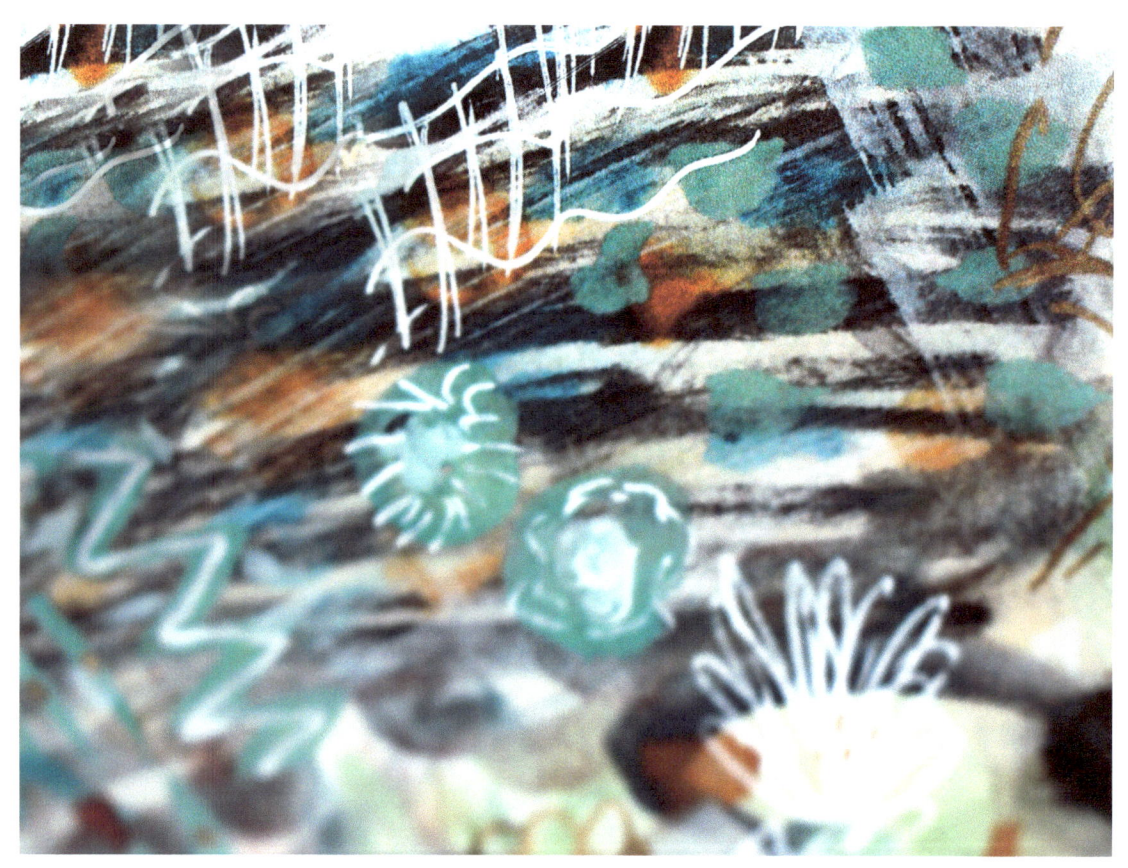

STORM

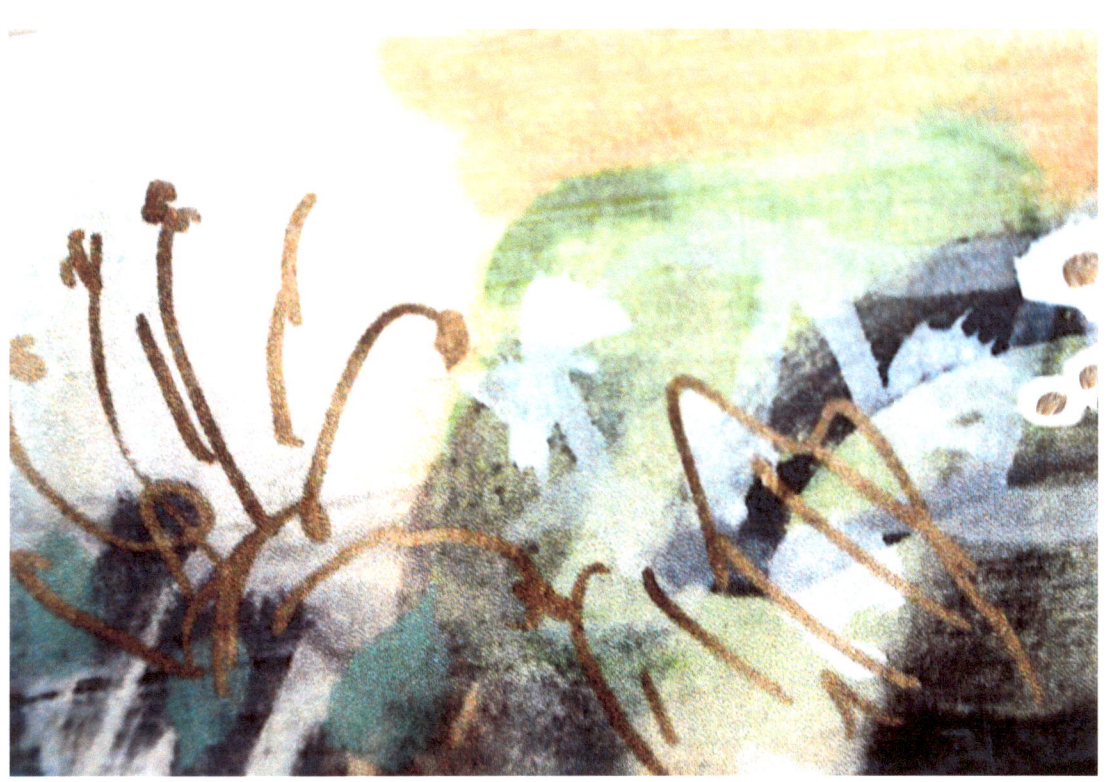

CLIFF

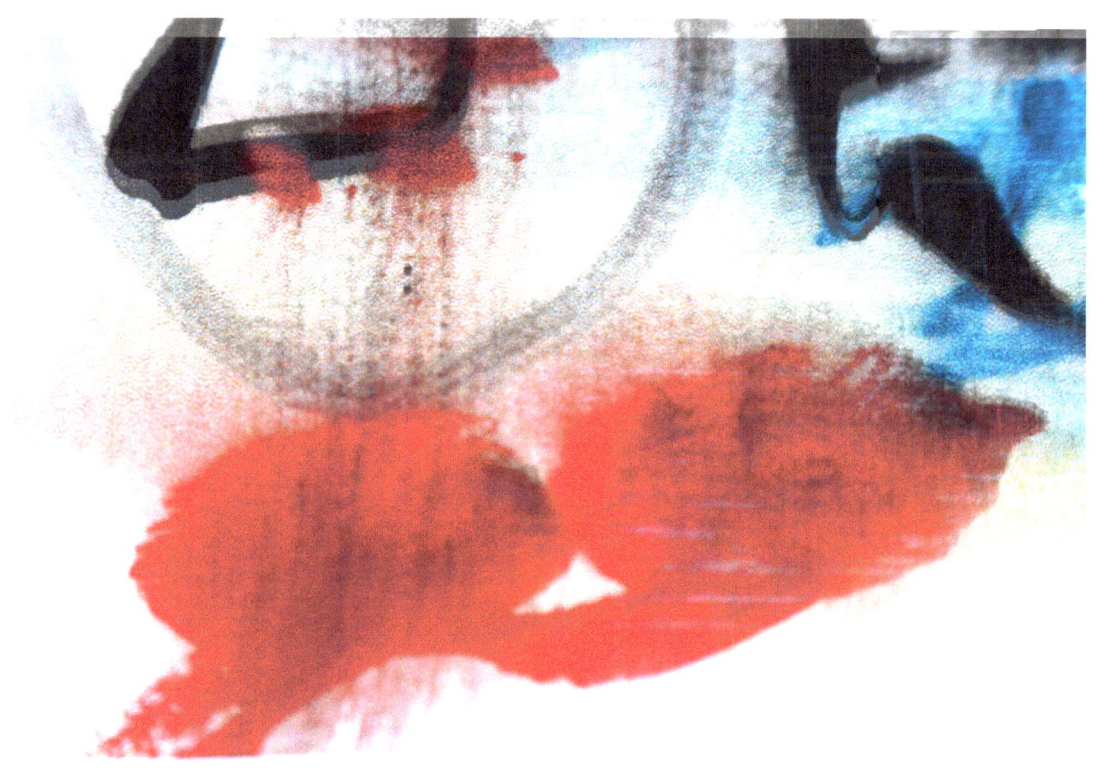

LOVERS
LOVERS

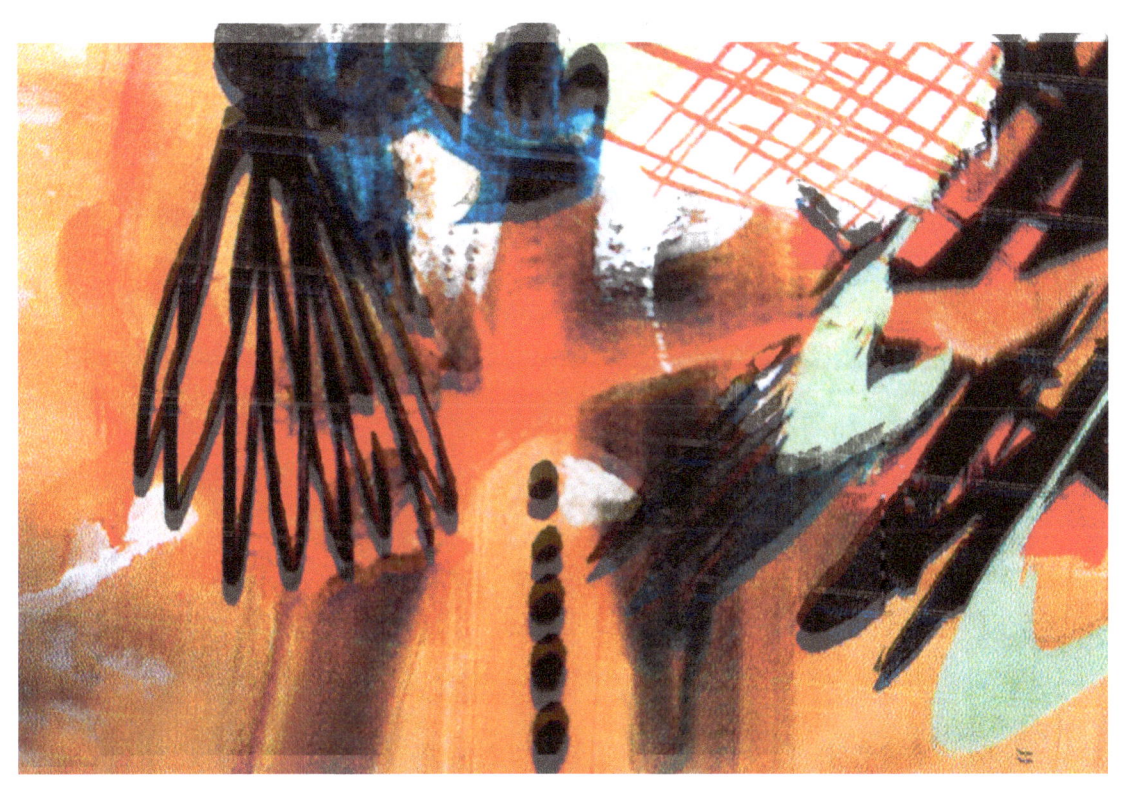

PENGUIN OBSERVING

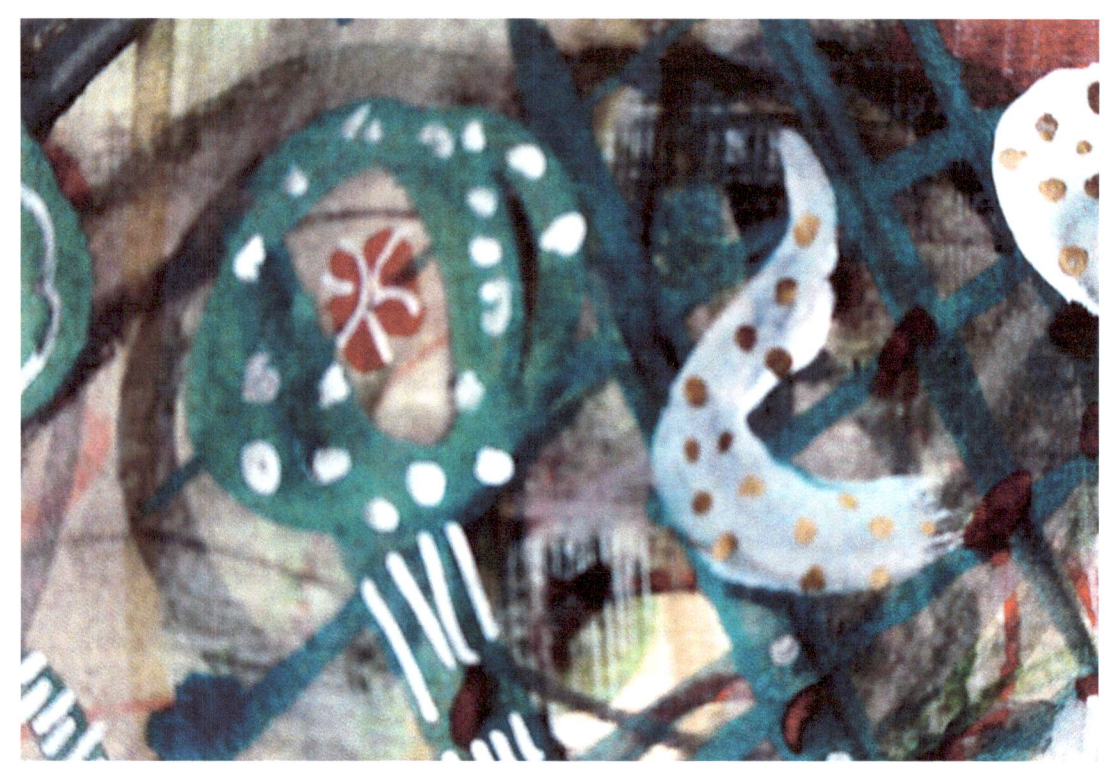

GHOST ESCAPING

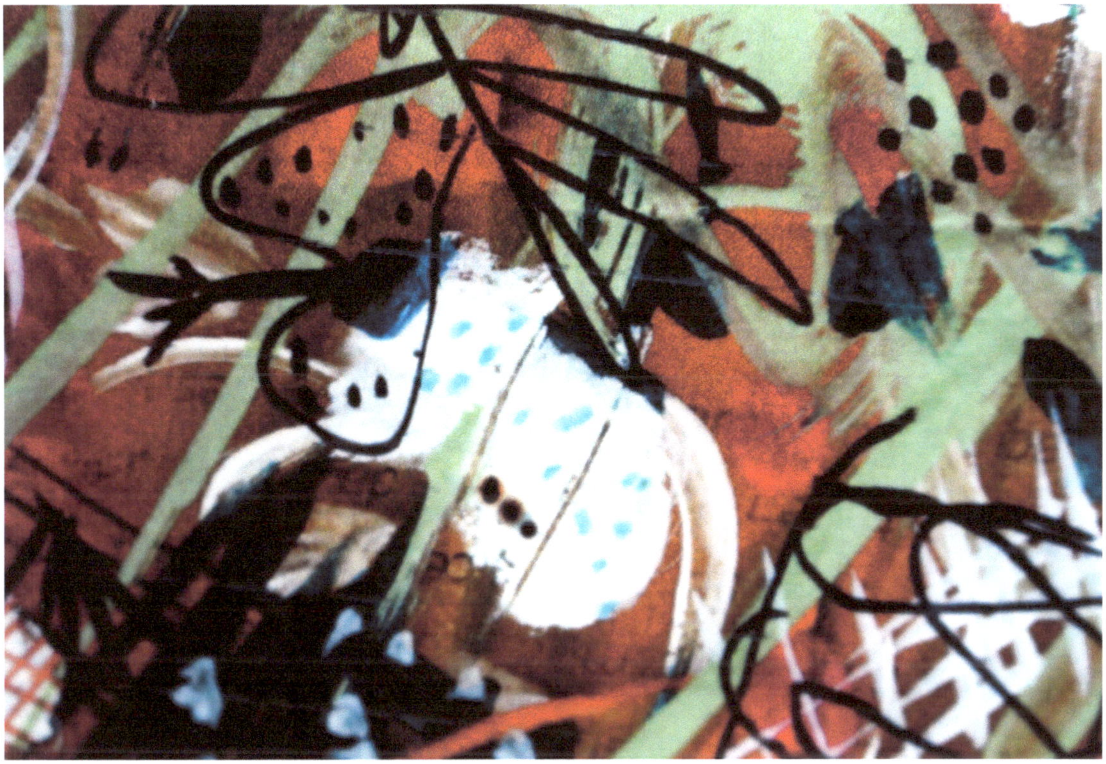

THE GARDEN OF FRIENDSHIP
"FRIENDS FOREVER"

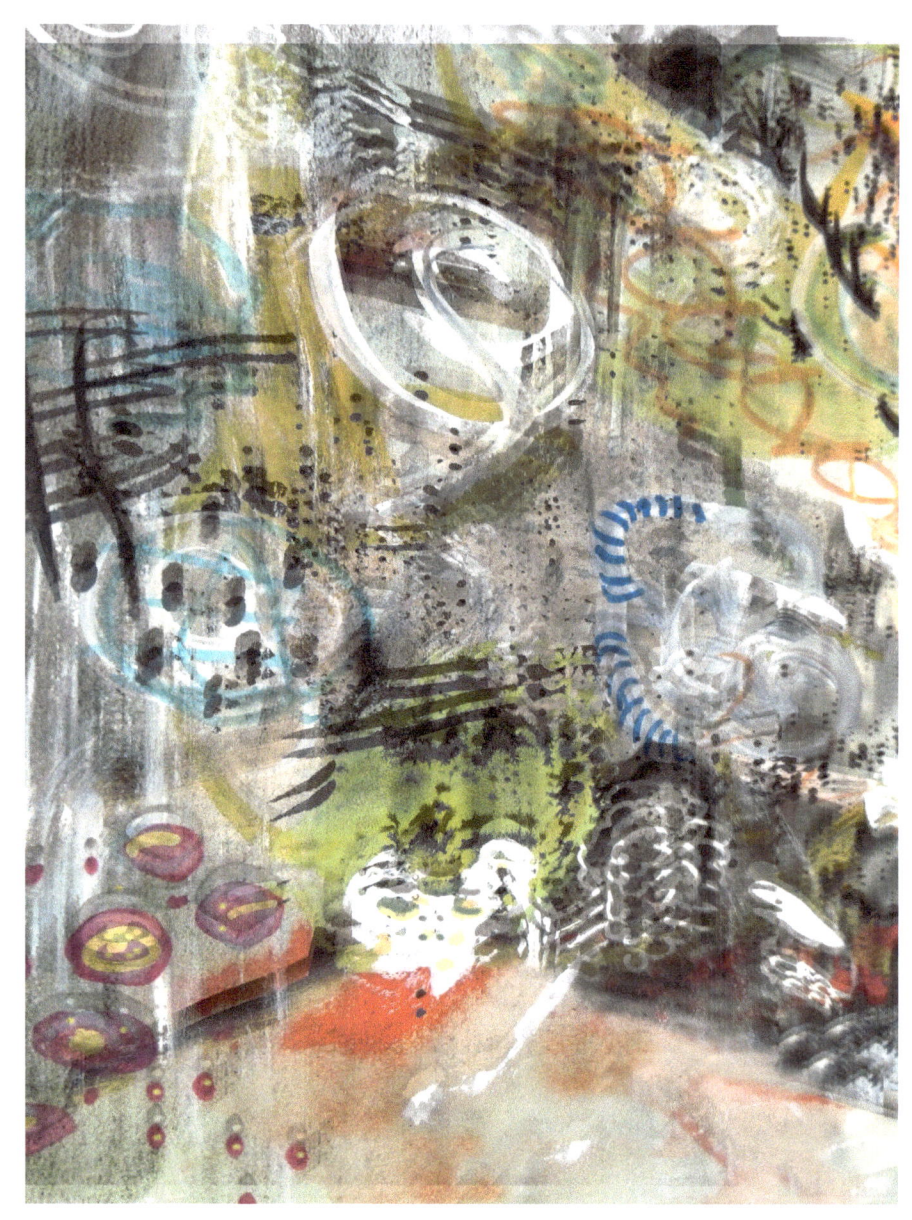

LIVING DEAD

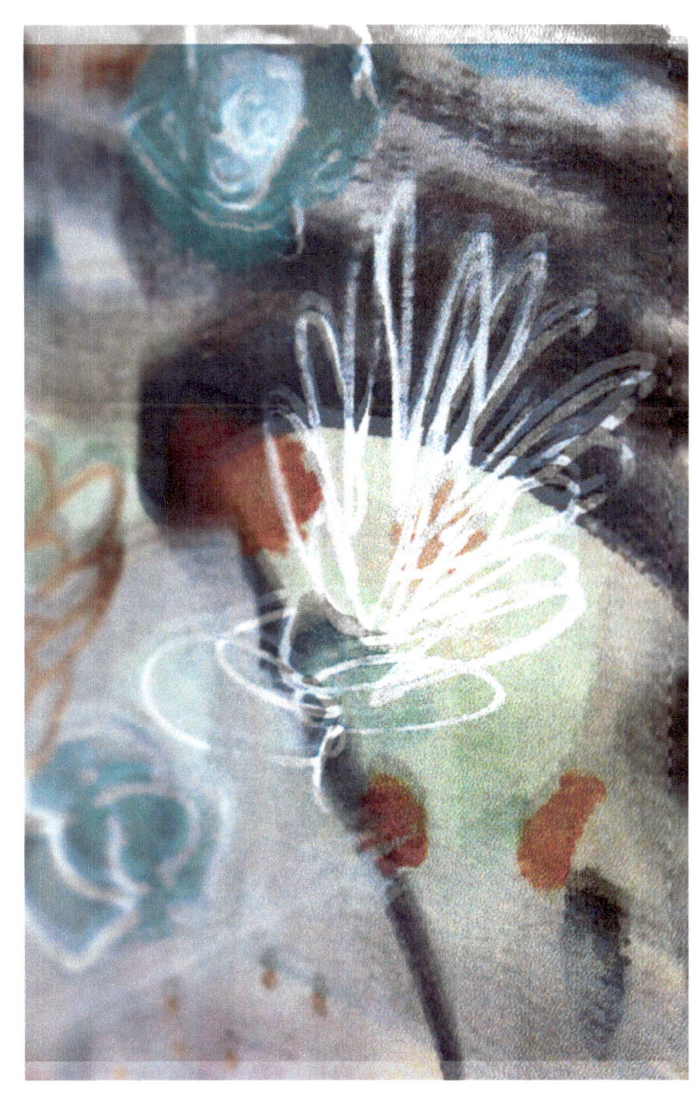

ROSE OF JERICHO
ROSE OF JERICHO

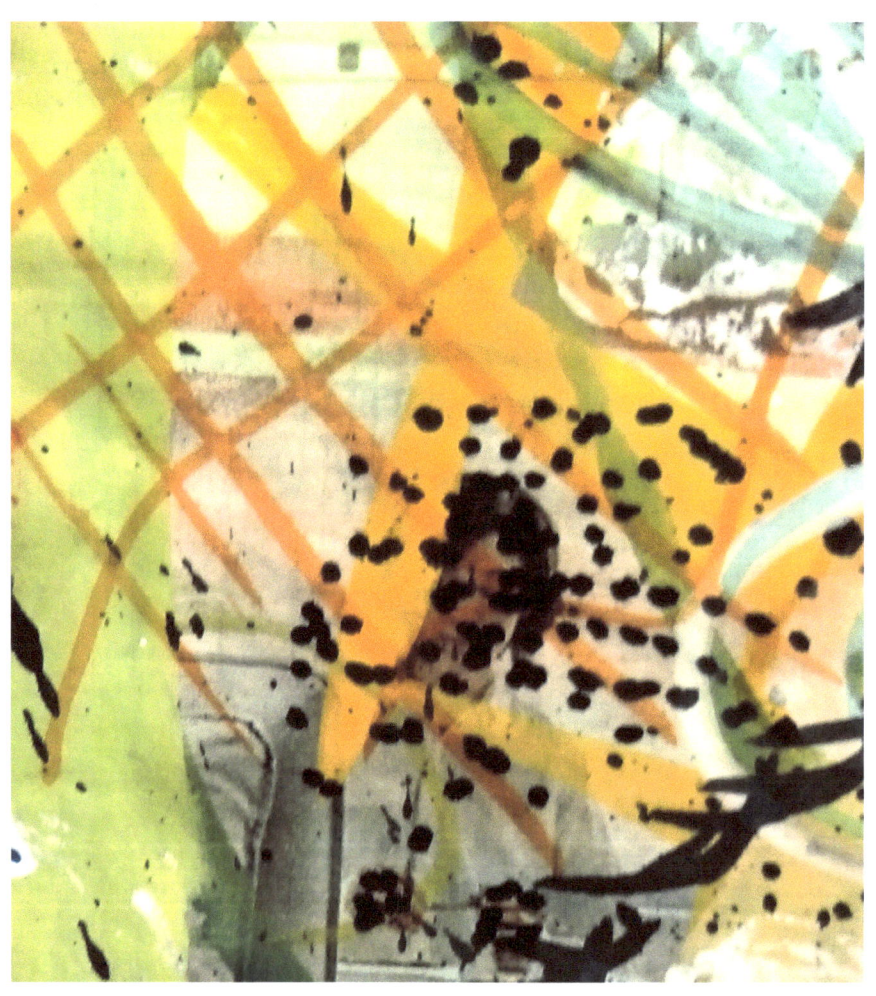

PAPAYA

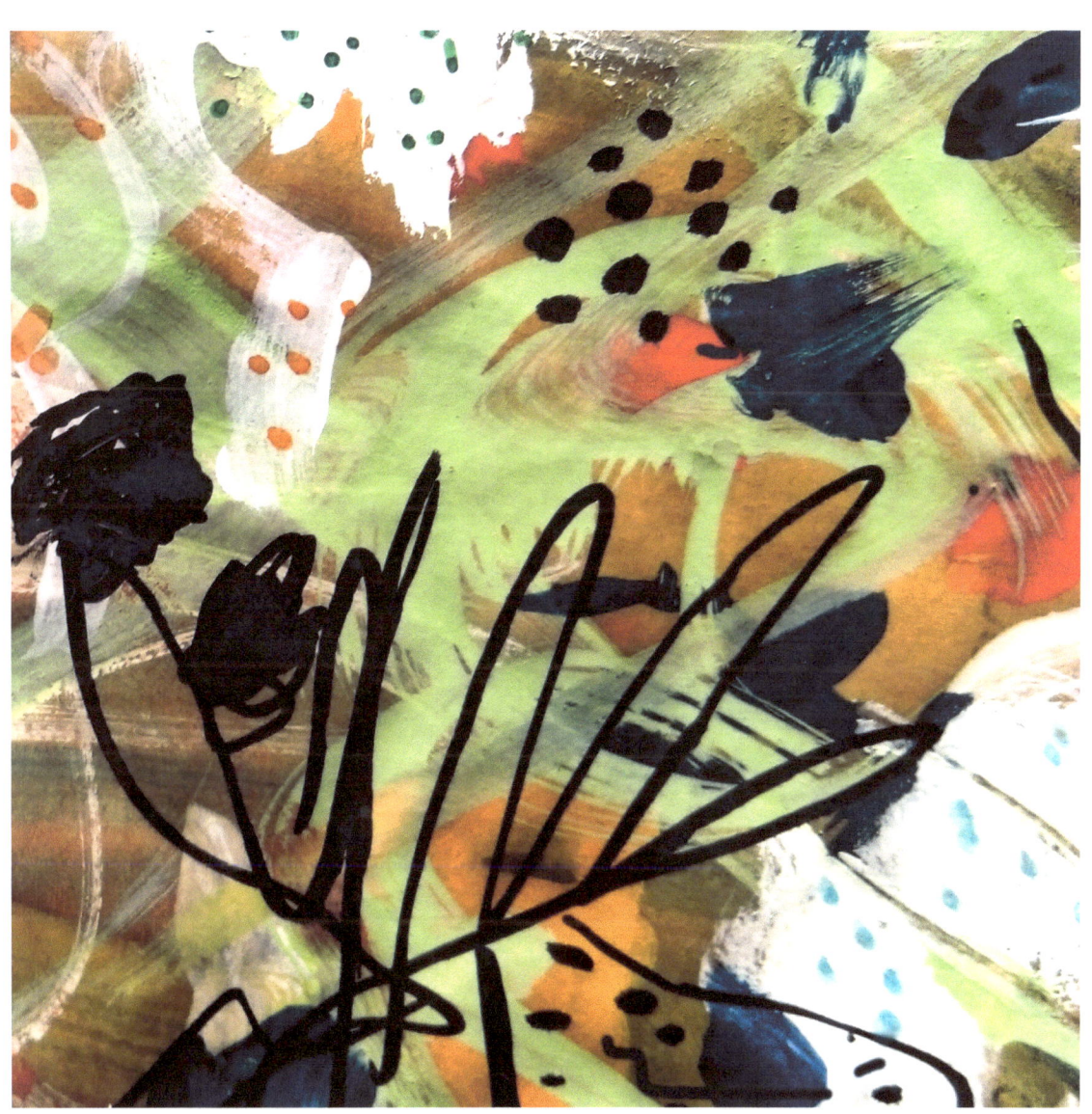

COLORFUL FISHES

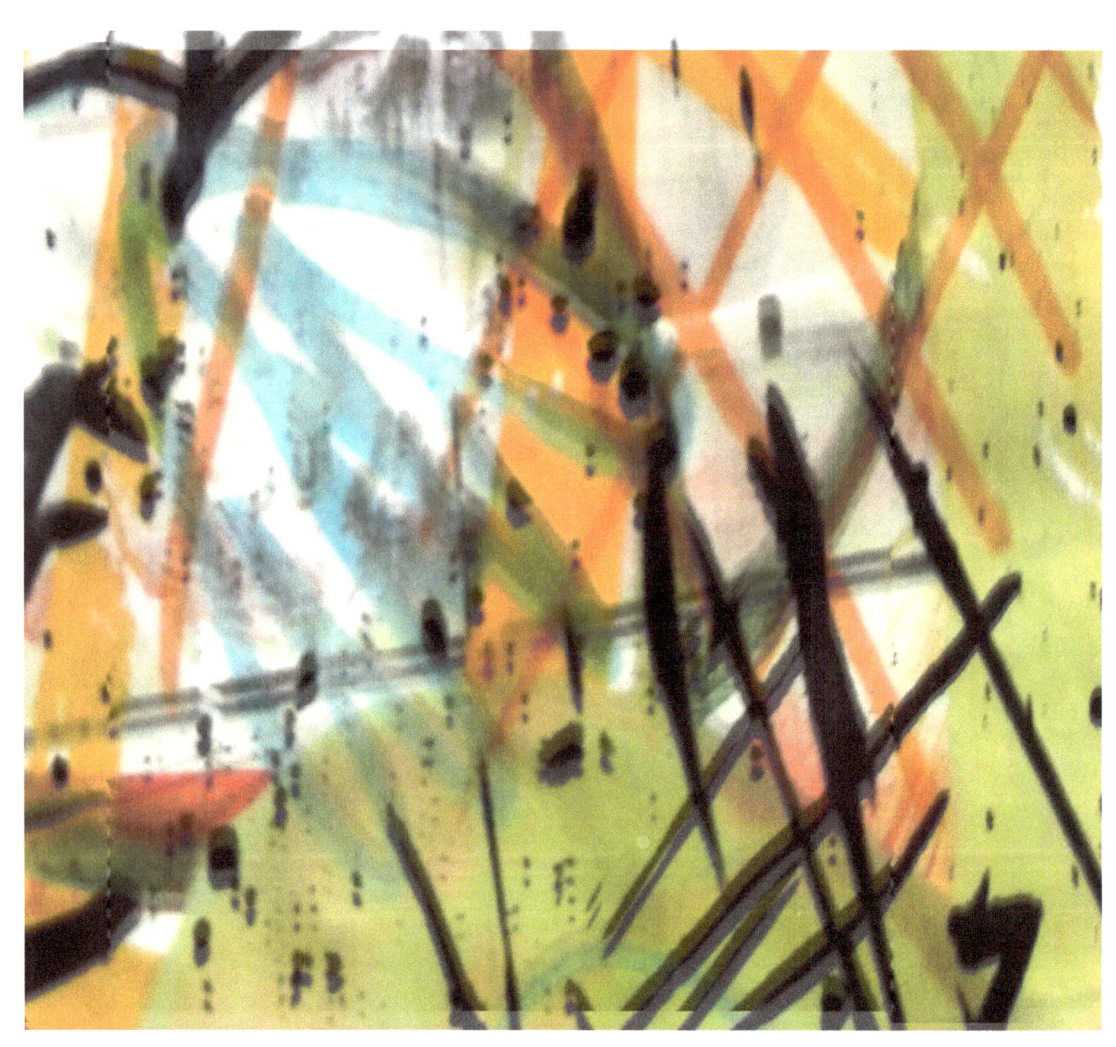

THE TROPICAL CORNER

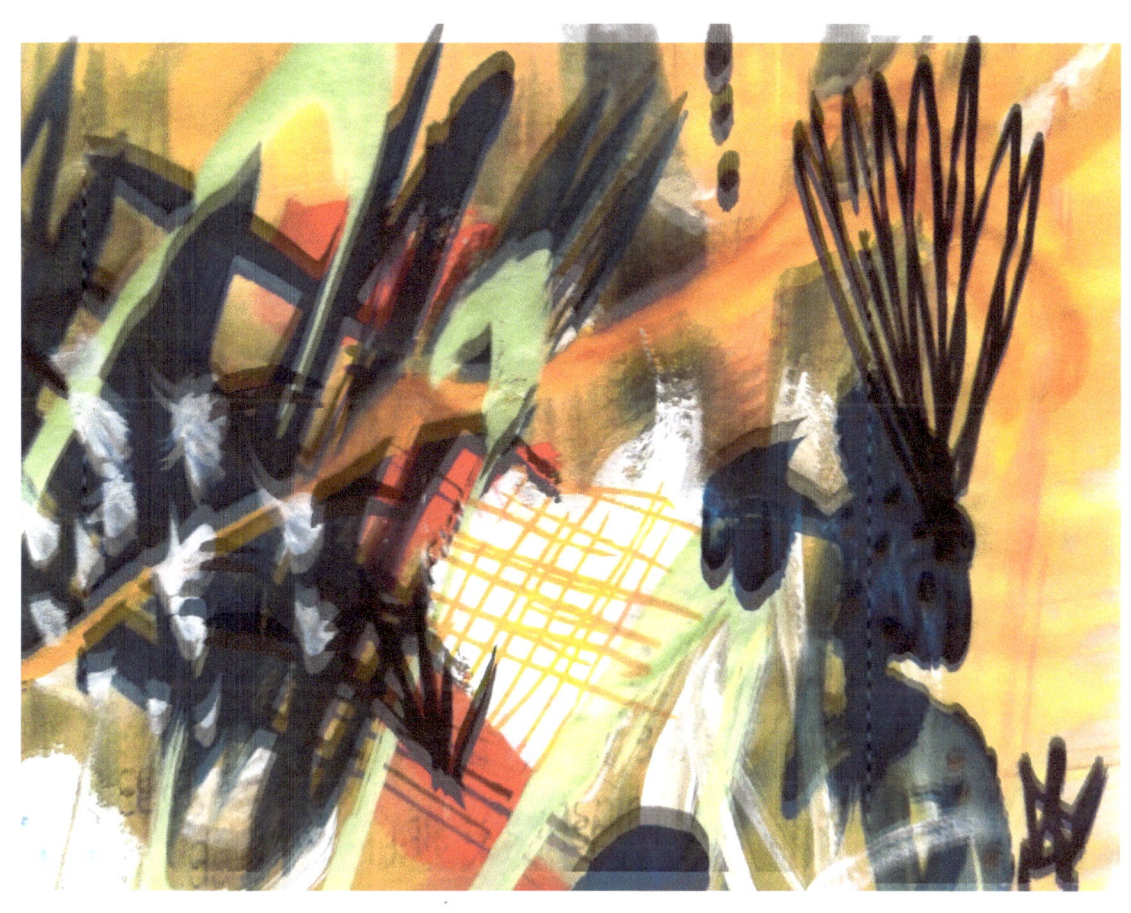

ROOSTER FISH

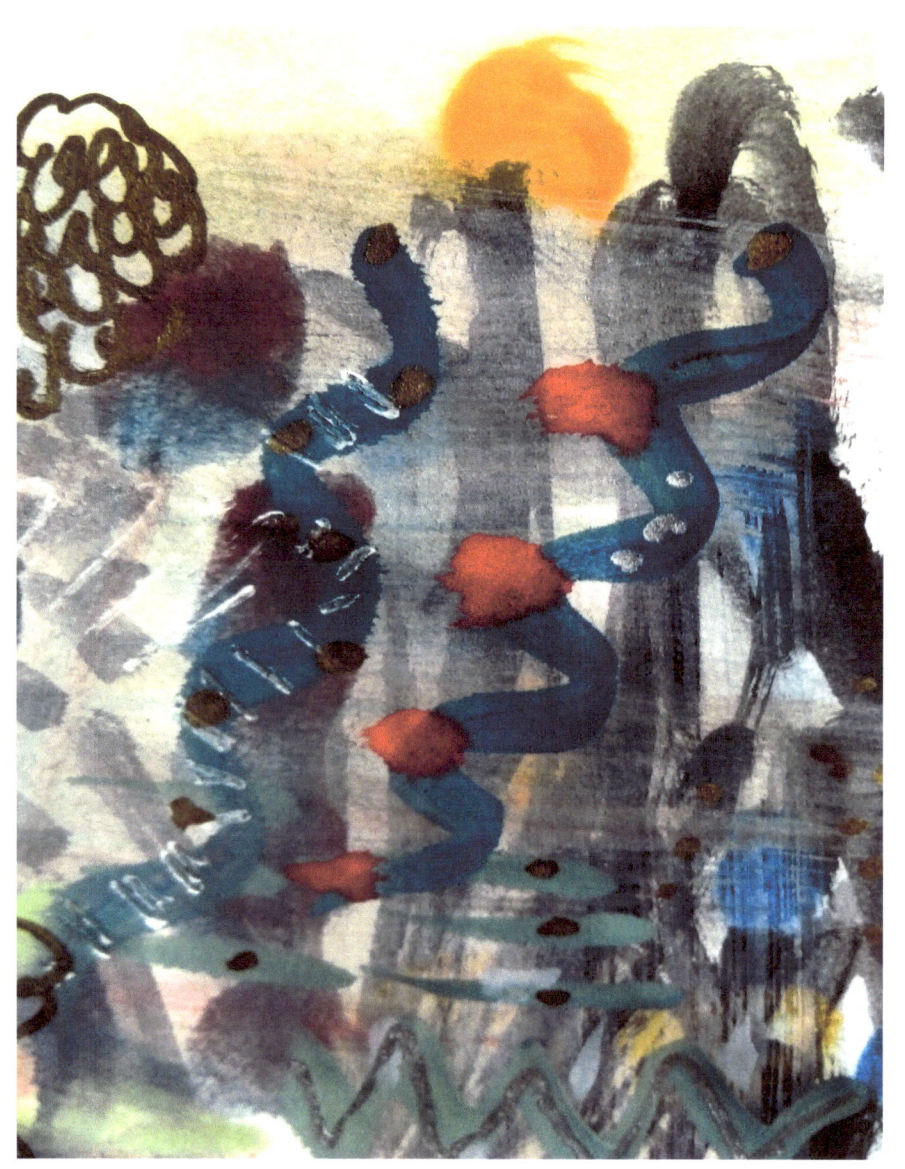

MARINE CITY

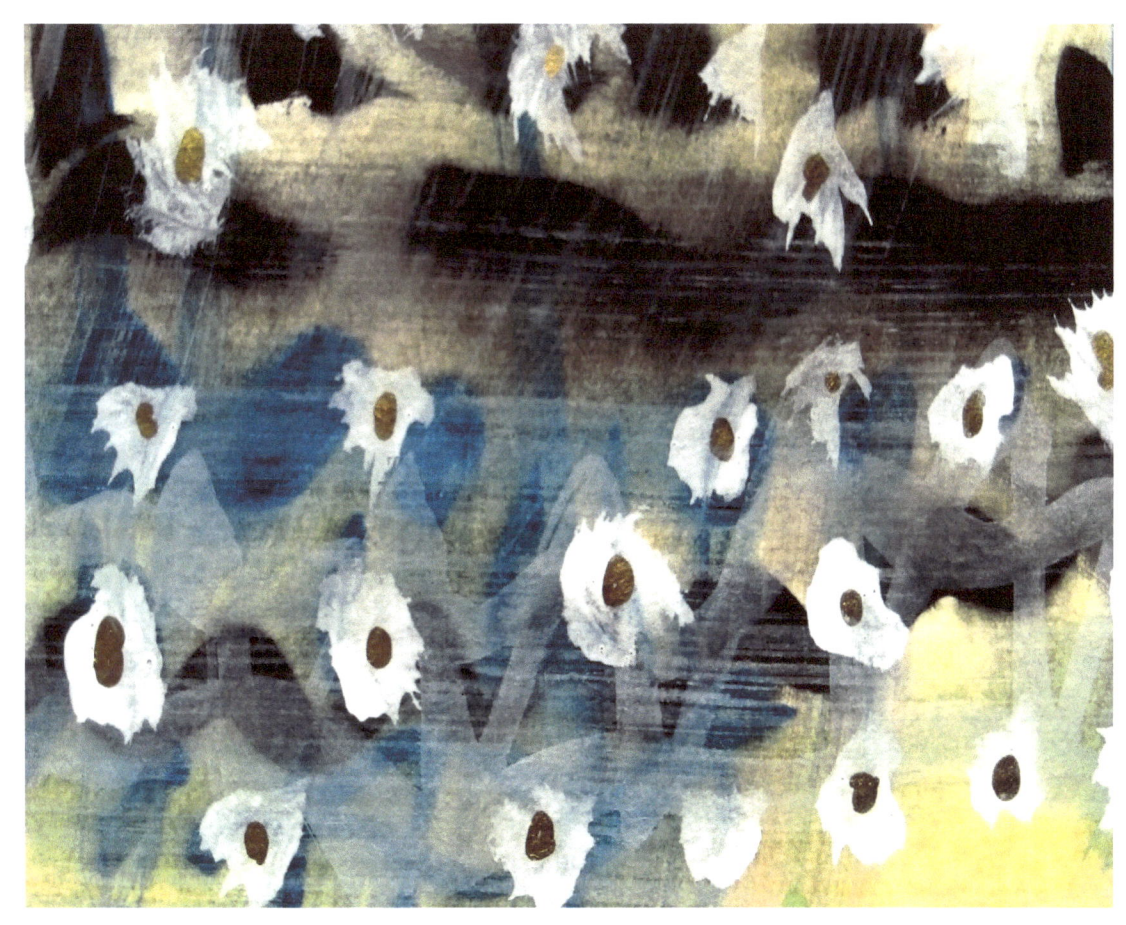

MAMMOTHS IN A DAISY
FIELD

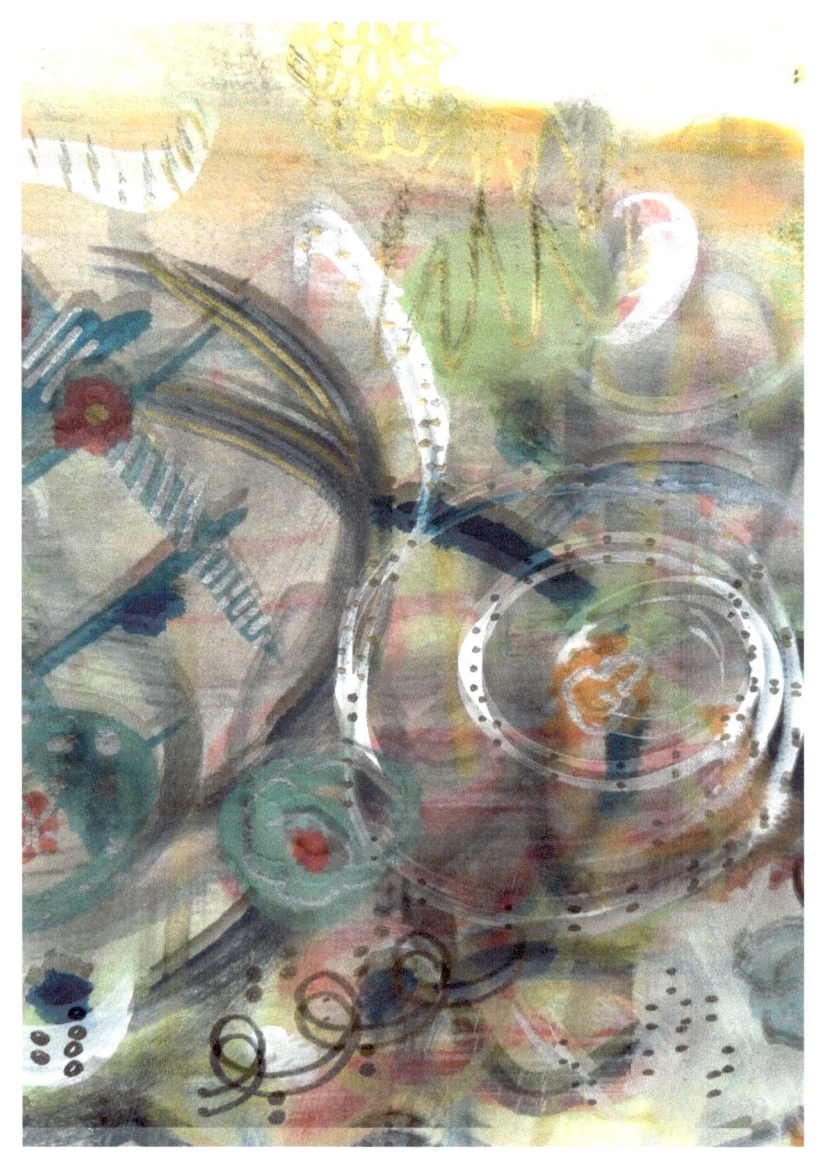

SPRING

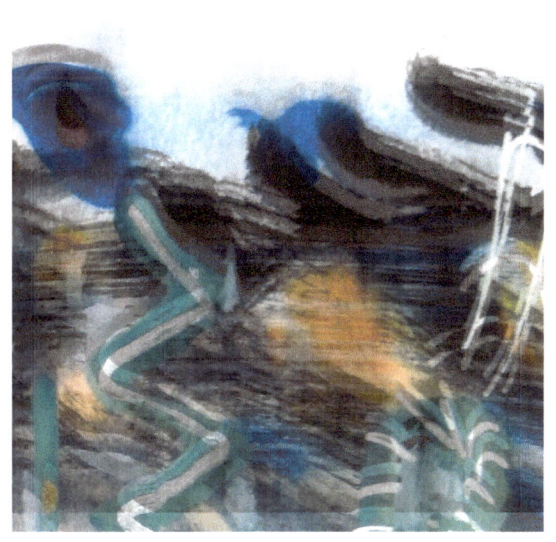

SPARROW
SPARROW

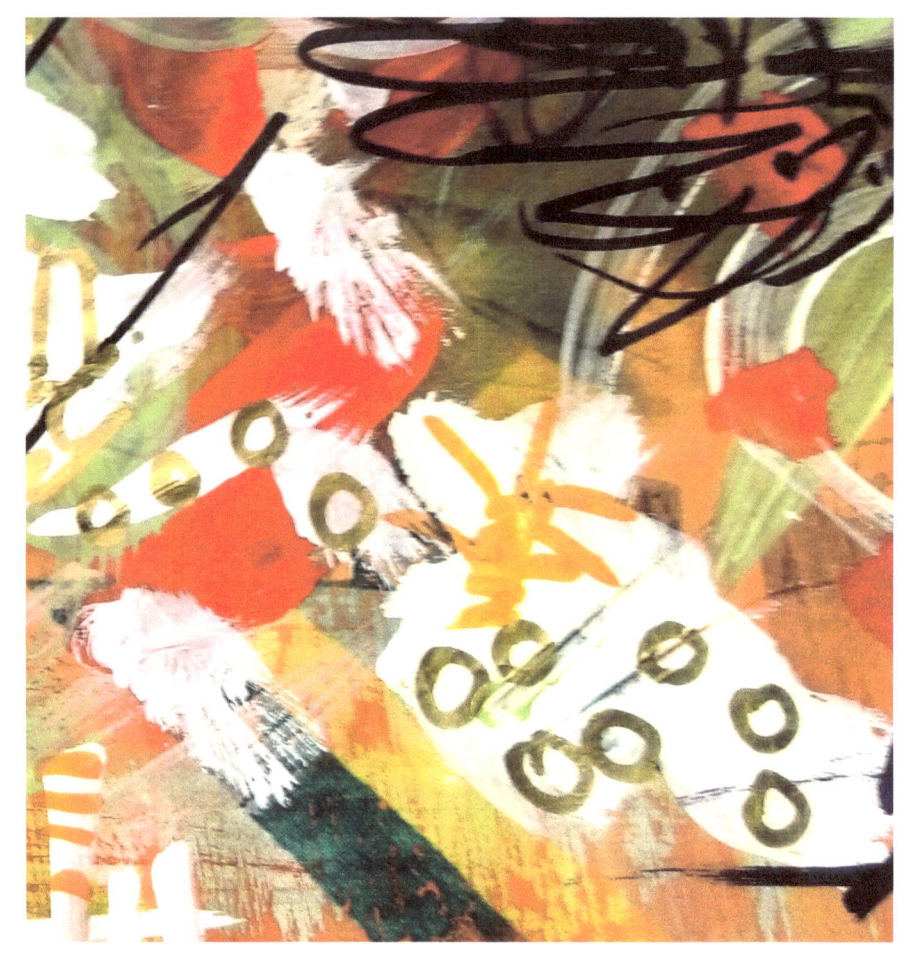

MOM NOÉL

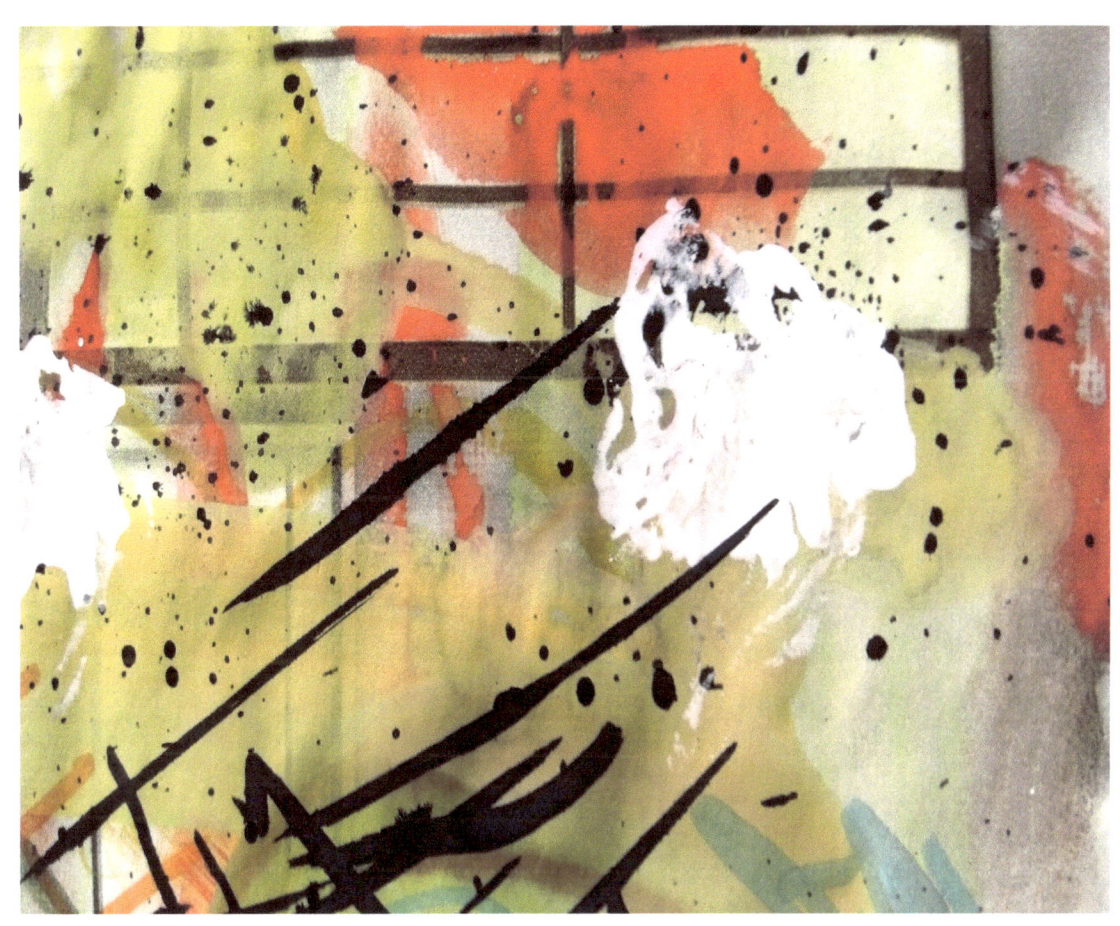

SHEEP IN THE WAR

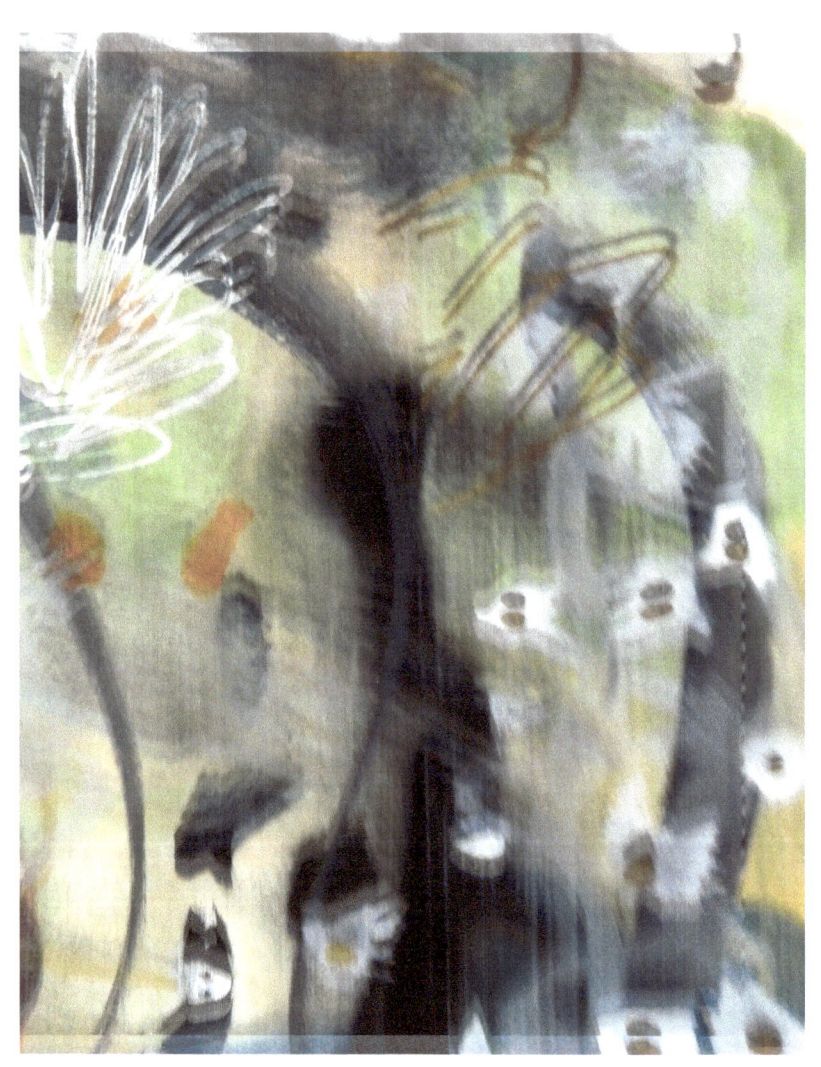

THE SHADOW
THE SHADOW

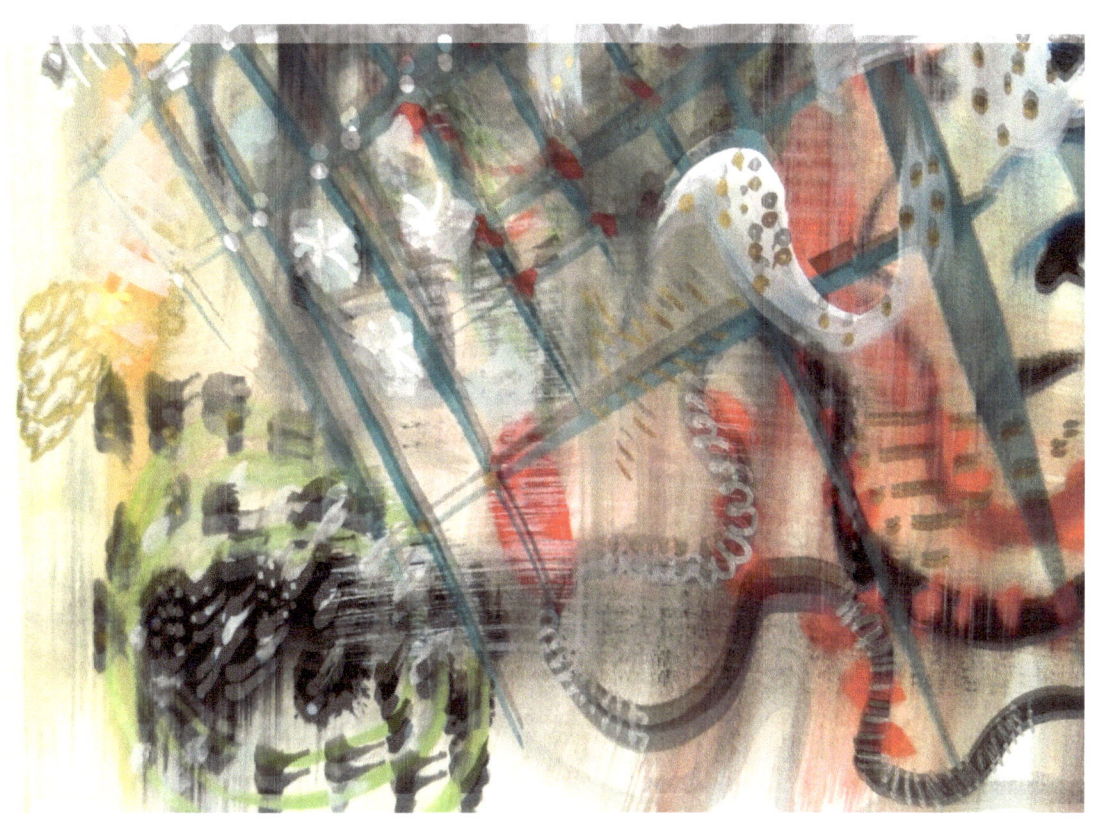

FEAR OF FREEDOM

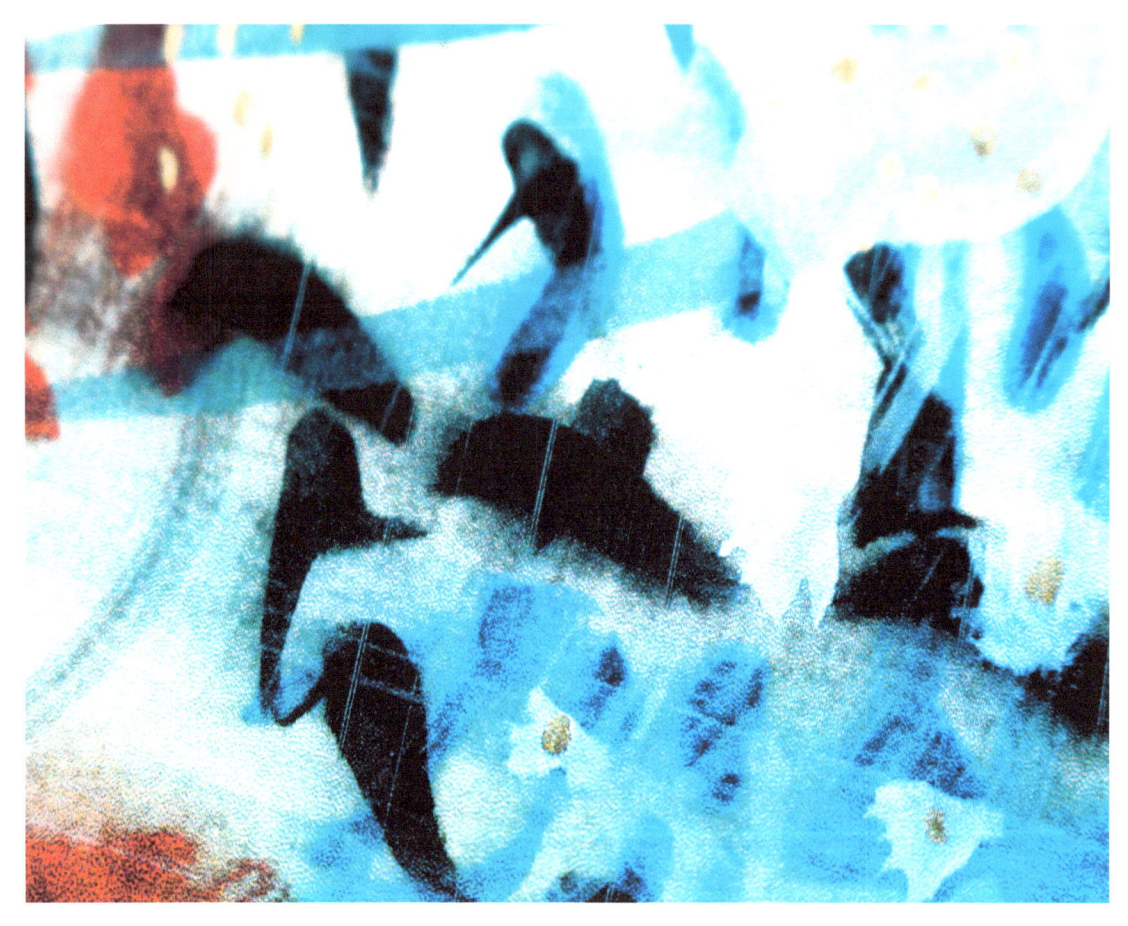

AQUATIC RED POPPIES & DOLPHINS

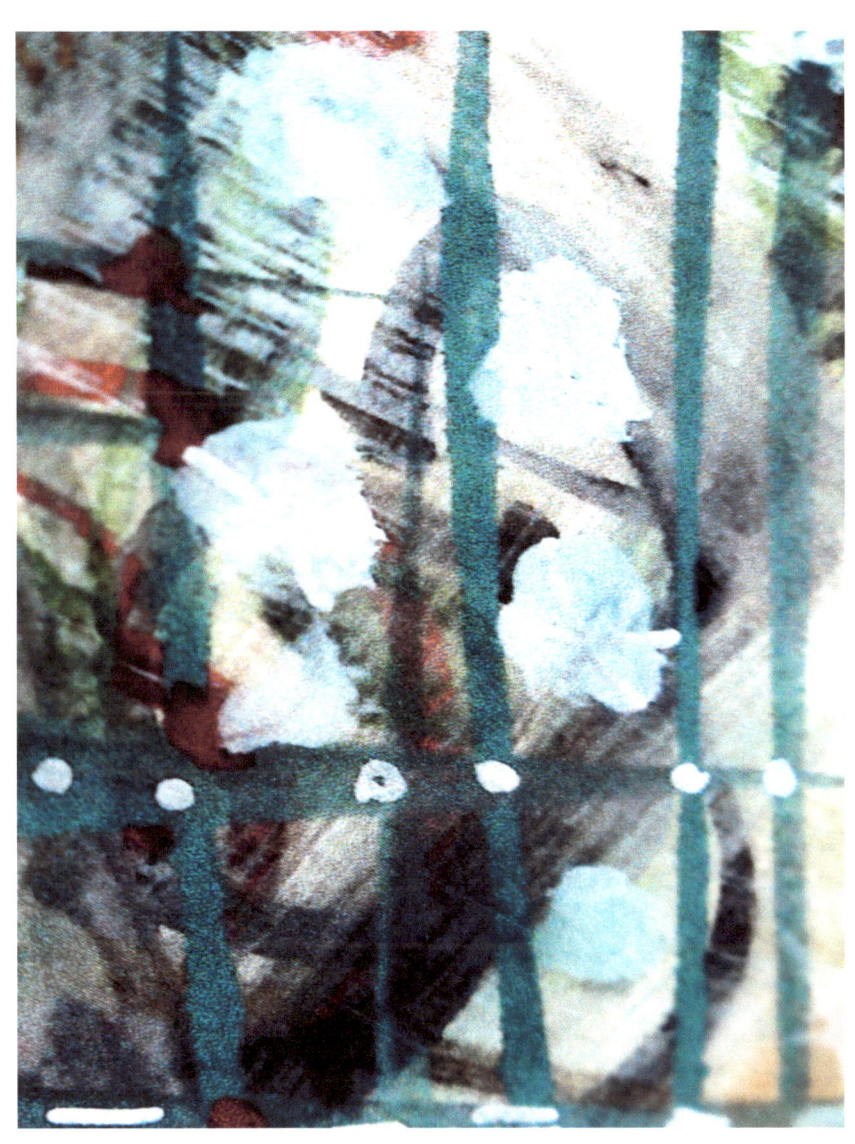

IMPRISONED ORCHIDS

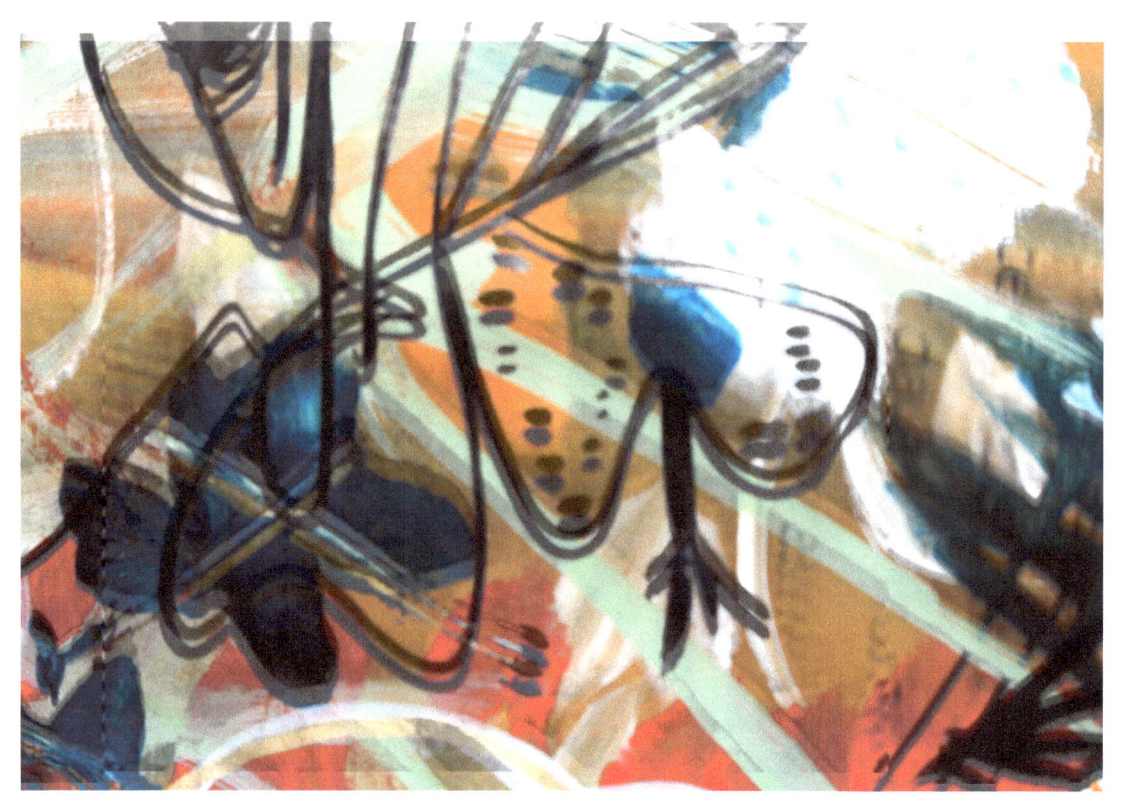

HEADLESS CHICKEN

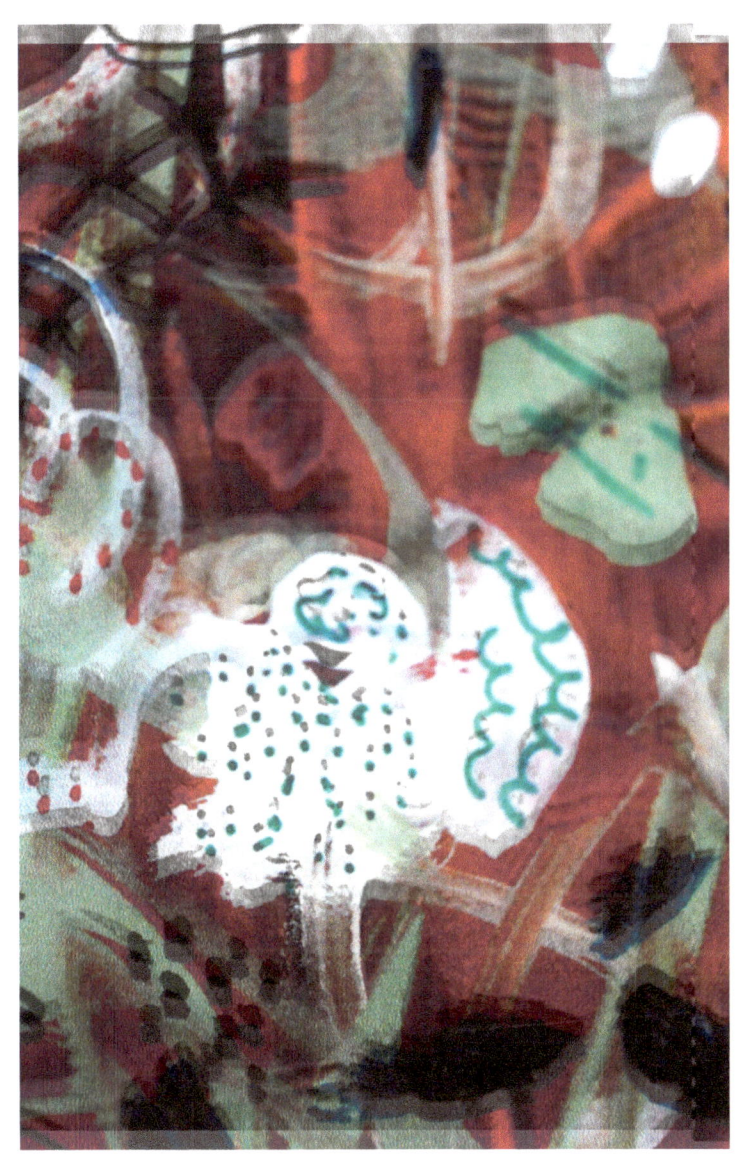

RUMBA OF FEATHERS
RUMBA OF FEATHERS

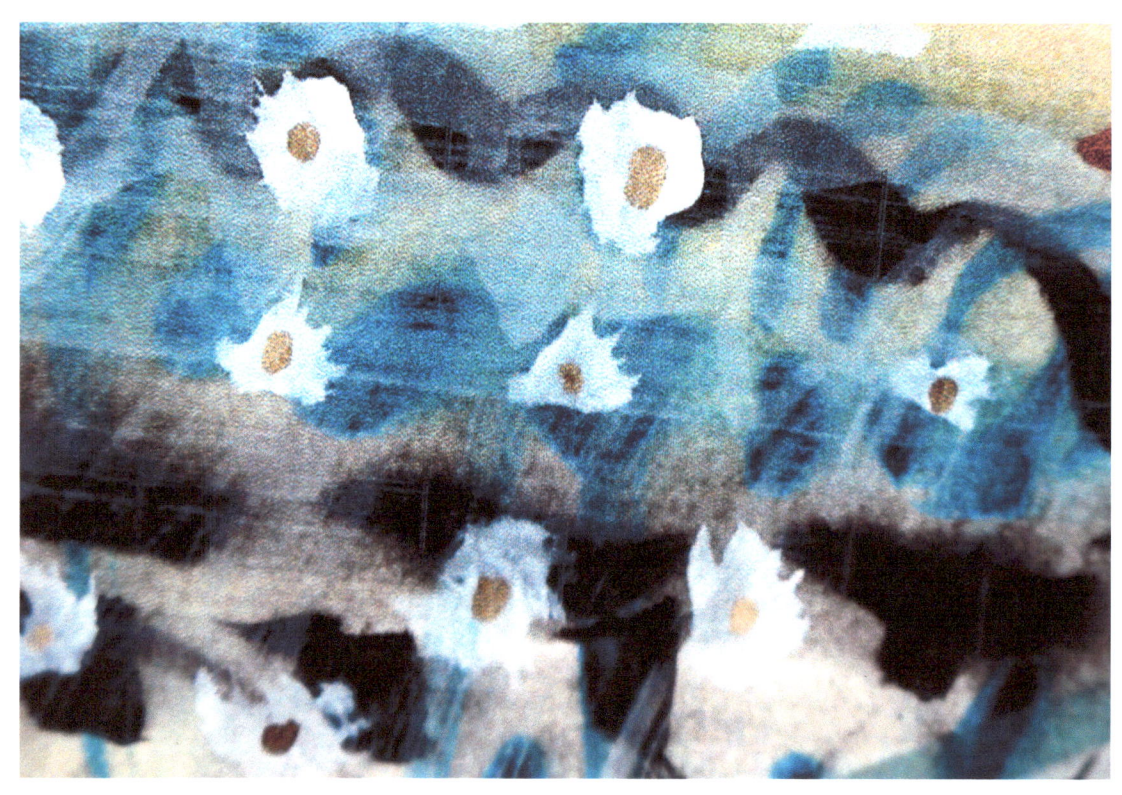

SEAGULLS & MARGARITAS ON THE BEACH

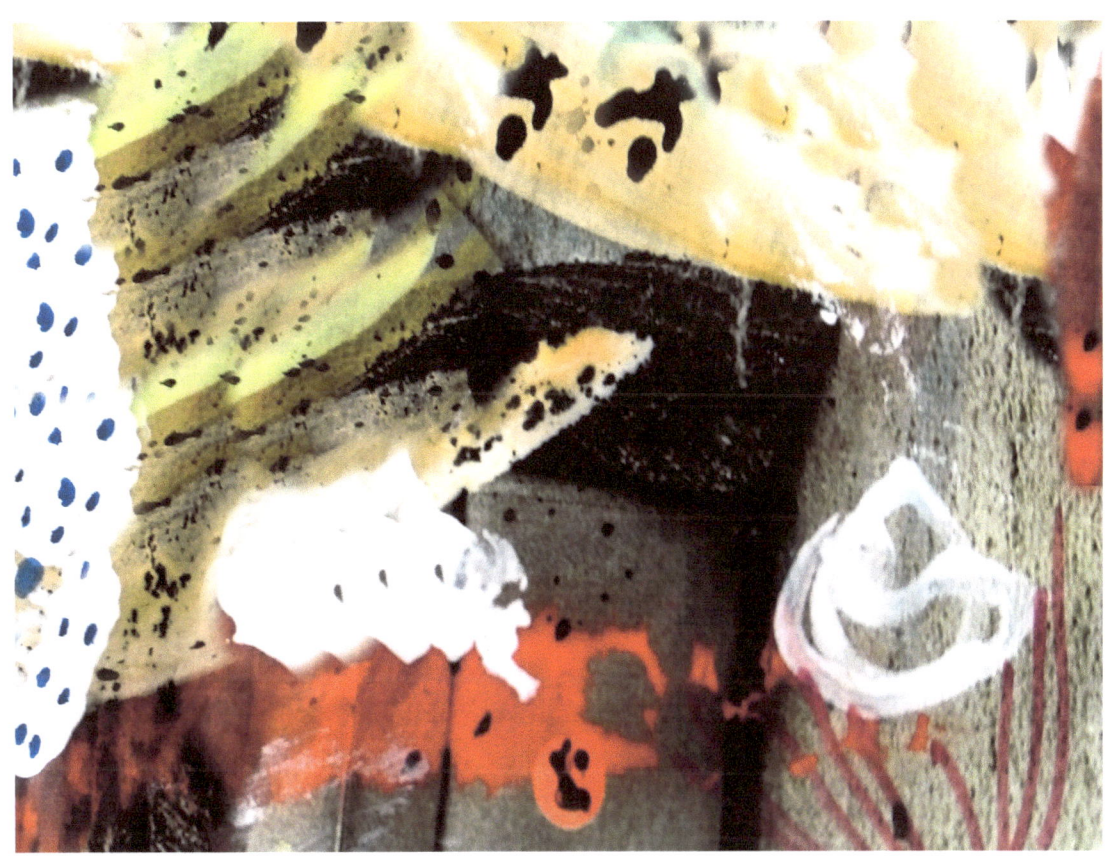

EYES

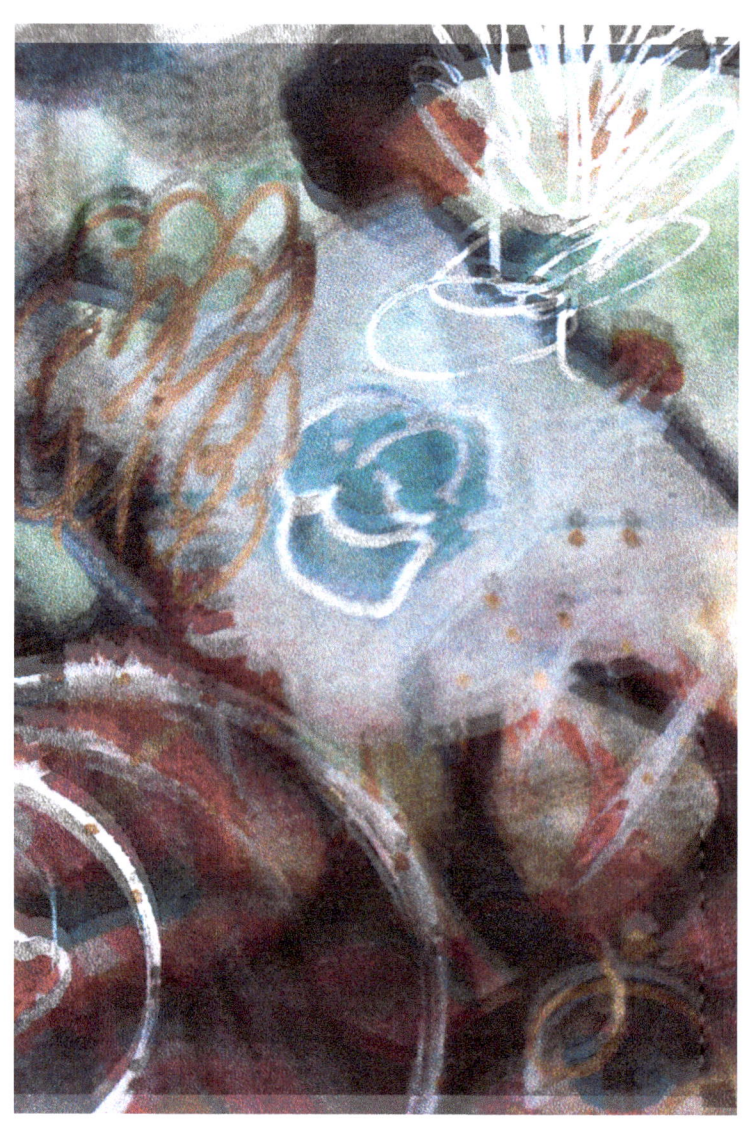

WINGED FLOWER
WINGED FLOWER

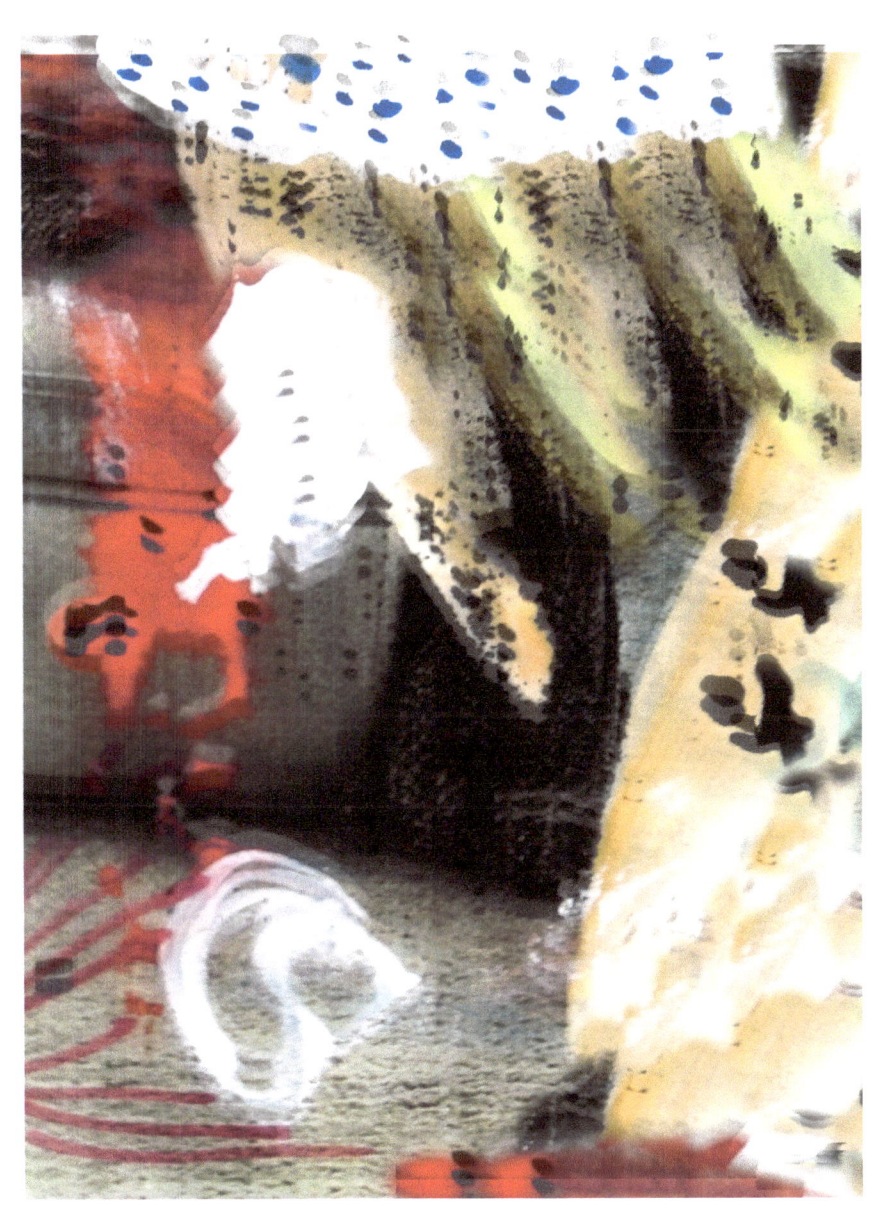

OUT OF THE ARMCHAIR

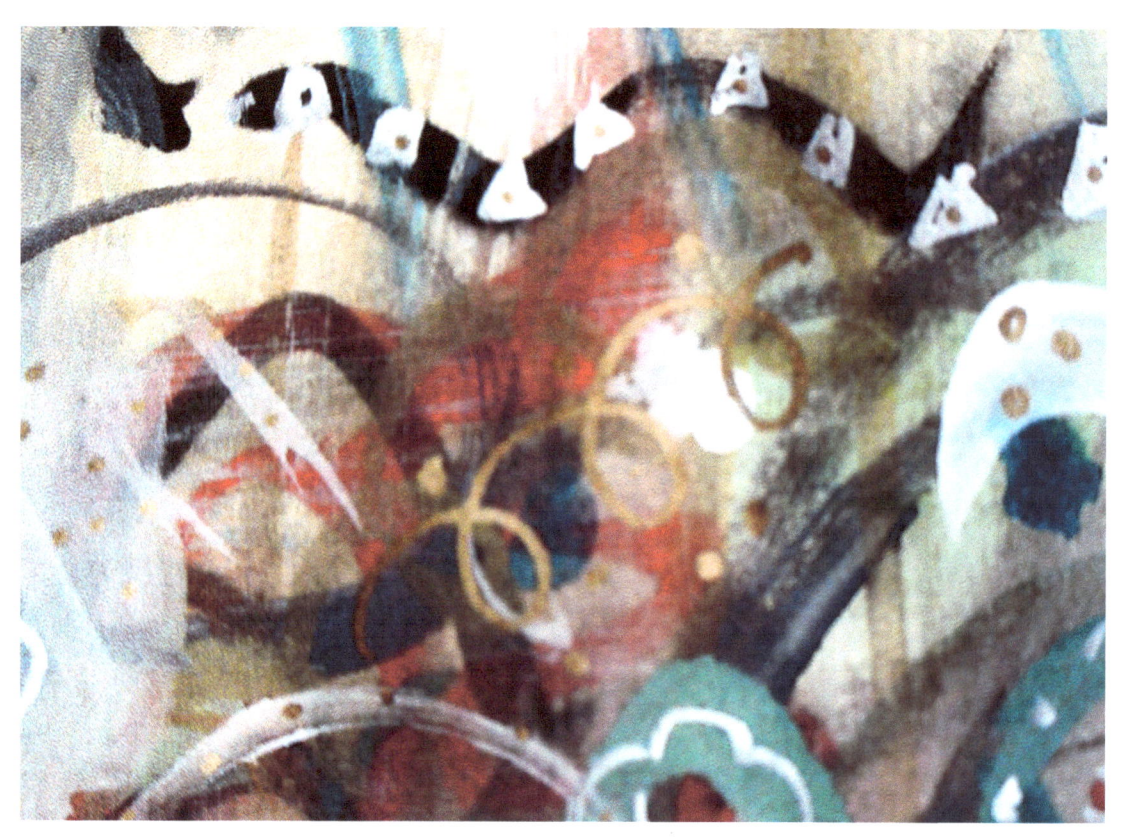

RUN THAT I CATCH YOU

As you can see the mind is wonderful, mysteriously versatile and flexible.

Maybe in a few days, when you go back to "The little book of the abstract universe", you will find very different meanings.

And that is ... our mind creates infinite realities and scenarios with the visual information we receive.

We can not ignore the influence of the moment through which our life goes through, what we have already lived or what we project in the future, therefore the meanings we can give to the images can vary substantially from observing them today and returning tomorrow.

All this is influencing, impacting and connecting with the heart to transform what we see and find a meaning to what is shown before our eyes.

Without looking for more meaning to what we see, no doubt, to observe is already food for the imagination and why not say it, in a certain way, a look at our complex inner world because we interpret from what has been learned, lived or seen previously conscious or unconsciously.

MARIAN MUÑOZ
graphic designer

Contact information

Mail
brandingesencial@gmail.com
pedidosbrandingesencial@gmail.com

web
www.brandingesencial.com

Follow me in
hastag: #brandingesencial

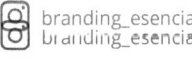 branding_esencial

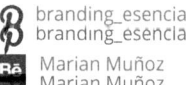 branding_esencial

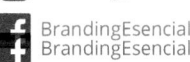 BrandingEsencial

Marian Muñoz

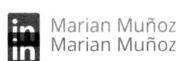 Marian Muñoz

www.ingramcontent.com/pod-product-compliance
Lightning Source LLC
Chambersburg PA
CBHW051925210526
45473CB00006B/2136